The RAGU BOLOGNESE COOKBOOK

Danny Bolognese

The RAGU BOLOGNESE COOKBOOK
The Secret Recipe and More

Danny Bolognese

Danny Bolognese

If you are poor and you make Bolognese, you're not really poor but Rich, for you've got Bolognese, and you know how to make it, one of the Great Treasures of the World, Ragu Bolognese. And no man who can make Ragu Bolognese can ever be poor, that's a fact. You've got Bolognese, you're are a King of Men.

DBZ

Broadway Fifth Press
New York, NY
Bolognese, The Secret Recipe and More
Copyright © 2015 by Danny Bolognese

All rights reserved. Printed in the United States of America.

No part of this book may be used or reproduced in any manner whatsoever without written permission except in the case of brief quotations embodied in critical articles and review.

First Edition
First Edition Broadway Fifth Press 2015
New York, New York
Cover Design Daniel Bellino-Zwicke
Cover photo property of Daniel Bellino Zwicke
First Published by Broadway Fifth Press 2015
New York, New York 10014

Library of Congress Cataloging-in-Publication Data, Bolognese, Danny
Bolognese, The Secret Recipe and More

ISBN – 13 : 978 - 1517150310
ISBN – 10 : 1517150310

1. Bolognese, Danny, Cooks – New York (State)—New York—Nonfiction, I Title

All Rights Reserved ...

Ragu Bolognese Cookbook

CONTENTS

Bolognese Sauce ... p. 12

Cookbookella ... p. 18

About Bolognese ... p. 20

Bolognese The Classic Recipe ... p. 21

Danny's Bolognese / Secret Recipe ... p. 24

Pasta Antipasto & More ... p. 30

Insalata Caprese ... p. 32

Italian Salad ... p. 34

Salad Dressing ... p. 37

Shrimp Cocktail ... p. 38

Antipasto Misti ... p. 39

Aspragus Parmigiano ... p. 42

Stuffed Zucchini ... p. 45

Zucchini Pie ... p. 47

Pickled String Beans ... p. 49

Baslamic Chicken Wings ... p. 51

Tomato Sauce ... p. 53

Marinara ... p. 55

Spaghetti Puttanesca ... p. 59

Spaghetti Pesto ... p. 61

Spaghetti Amatriciana ... p. 63

CONTENTS

Pasta w/ Mushroom Sauce ... p. 66

Fusilli Siciliana ... p. 70

Lasagna ... p. 72

Lasagna Bolognese ... p. 78

Meatballs ... p. 81

Rigatoni w/ Sausage ... p. 84

Pasta w/ Rabbit Ragu ... p. 87

Fettuccine Alfredo ... p. 90

Pasta Cacio Pepe ... p. 91

Pasta w/ Artichokes Tomato & Peas ... p. 93

Maccheroni w/ Mushroom Veal Ragu ... p. 95

Bucatini Michelangelo ... p. 98

Rigatoni w/ Ossobuco Ragu ... p. 100

Maccheroni w/ Pork Ragu ... p. 102

Maccheroni w/ Sausage & Peas ... p. 105

Sausage Meatballs w/ Rice ... p. 107

Lentil Soup ... p. 109

Sicilian Chicken & Vegetable Soup ... p. 113

Minestrone alla Genovese ... p. 116

Garlic Oregano Chicken ... p. 118

John's Secret Chicken Cacciatore ... p. 120

CONTENTS

Pollo Zingaro ... p. 123

Pork Milanese ... p. 125

Porchetta ... p. 128

Steak & Onions ... p. 131

Steak Pizzaiola ... p. 133

Chicken Francese ... p. 135

Sicilian Chicken ... p. 137

Veal & Peppers ... p. 140

London Broil Italian Style ... p. 142

Roast Tuscan Potatoes ... p. 144

Roast Peppers ... p. 145

Eggs & Sandwiches ... p. 146

Salami & Egg ... p. 147

Asparagus Frittata ... p. 149

Fried Mortadella ... p. 152

The Danny Special ... p. 154

The Italian Hot Dog ... p. 155

Ricotta Cheesecake ... p. 158

Tiramisu ... p. 160

Torta Caprese ... p. 163

Budino ... p. 165

Party Bolognese .. p. 168

Ragu Bolognese Cookbook

BOLOGNESE SAUCE ... *"It's Oh So Good!"*

Bolognese Sauce. You gotta just love it. It's one of the greatest things ever, oh-so-tasty and soul satisfying. Do you know it? Have you ever tasted the *Real Thing*? Well here it is, in all its glory and wonderfulness that is a *properly* made Ragu Bolognese, rich, lush, *Soul Satisfying* and oh so *fantastic, i*t's *Bolognese*! Sorry I'm going on-and-on, but that's the affect this wonderful thing called the Bolognese, has on one. It's just so delightful and *blissfully delicious*, one can't but extoll its awesome virtues, It's Bolognese! So, whether you've ever had the real thing or not, here it is. If you are one who has tasted a properly made Bolognese then *you must now be in love with it*, that's a given with its incredibly fabulous taste, you no doubt crave it all the time. Well *now you can make*. This recipe of which I was taught to make form my former boss Chef Pasquale when I was working as a cook some 25 years ago.

If you are poor and you make Bolognese, you can never really be poor, but Rich, for you've got Bolognese. You know how to make it, for it's truly one of the Great Treasures of the World, the Ragu Bolognese. And no man who can make Bolognese can ever be poor. That's a fact, you've got Bolognese, *you're a King of Men.*

I went to culinary school in New York. We were taught how to cook Classic French Cuisine. I loved it, cooking French Food, eating it, going to French restaurants and studying this great cuisine. Our textbooks were from two great French Master Chefs, Louis Diat and Auguste Escoffier. We started from the beginning and learned how to make the classic mother sauces according to Escoffier and The Escoffier Cookbook. We learned all the great classical French dishes and it was wonderful. The summer after my first year I got a job at what was at the time the undisputable greatest restaurant in New York, Lutece, owned and run by the greatest French Chef in America at the time, Andre Soltner. Mr. Soltner interviewed and hired me personally. That was quite a feat and I was honored and very proud. His kitchen was run in the classic French manner of cooking and learning how to cook French Food, you start at the bottom and work your way up and through all the different stations, and that's what I did, I started at the bottom there at Lutece prepping vegetables, cutting carrots, potatoes, and turnips into juliennes and batonettes or turning the veggies into little football-like shapes one-by-one. This was all tedious work, but the vegetables looked great on the plate alongside a perfectly cooked piece of fish with a Buerre Blanc or some other classic French Sauce napping it. Yes Lutece was not only at the time the # 1 French Restaurant in New York but the # 1 Top Best of all restaurants in the city. It was also considered the best restaurant in the country and I was working there. This was a big deal.

Danny Bolognese

What's that you say, I thought we were talking about Bolognese here, what's all this talk of French Food and Lutece? Isn't Ragu Bolognese Italian you say? Yes, correct, but hold on, I'm getting to it, and soon we will leave French Cuisine behind and move on to Italian Food and that wonderfully fabulous thing know as Ragu Bolognese, or as they say in America Bolognese Sauce, or simply Bolognese.

Well I'm Italian. Italian-American that is, or more specifically a Sicilian-American. All the great food that my mother and aunts cooked for me, we never had a Bolognese. We were Sicilian and Neapolitan, we didn't make or eat Bolognese. We ate Tomato Sauce, Marinara, and most important of all, Sunday Sauce, otherwise known as *Gravy*. These were sauces of the south and that's what we ate, not Bolognese, that was from the north, of Bologna and Emilia Romagna the region that the great city of Bologna is part of, and some would say that Ragu Bolognese is more like a French Food as compared to the sauces and the ragu's of the south. Like French Food, a Ragu Bolognese is quite rich, getting its richness by simmering the meat with tomatoes and red wine for quite a long time (3 hours). No, they never made Bolognese in my family, and I never even had this great dish until I was way into my 20's. My aunts made the most wonderful Sunday Gravy, laden with Sausages, Meatballs, and Braciole, but never a Bolognese. They made Tomato Sauce and Marinara, staples of Italian Cooking and of the south. The closest thing we ever had to a

Bolognese was the Ragu al Sicilian that my mother made with ground beef and tomatoes (no wine) simmering together. This ragu is much like a Bolognese but not nearly as rich, a result of not having any wine in it and not cooking as long.

OK, so how did I learn how to make Bolognese. We're gonna back track a little and you will know. So I was into French Cuisine and wanted to become a chef. I went to culinary school and got a job for a few months at Lutece, and I learned a few things, but what I learned most was that working in restaurant kitchens was hard and demanding work. From Lutece I then went on to work with the King of Nouvelle Cuisine in New York at The Palace Restaurant with Chef Michelle Fitoussi. After working with Chef Fitoussi for 2 years I went on to work with the late great Patrick Clarke at the Odeon, another top French Restaurant of the time. After my one year stint at the Odeon I got my first Sous Chefs job at Woods Restaurant on Madison Avenue up near 64th Street and all the expensive high priced Boutique Clothing stores and what not. Woods was a very good eclectic-cuisine restaurant that catered to *The Ladies Who Lunch*, and it was the first restaurant that I got to do my own food, as the chef let me do the daily specials. Woods was another great experience on my way to becoming a chef. I

I took my first trip to Italy in 1985, seeing Rome, Florence, Naples, Venice, and the Amalfi Coast, it was wonderful and quite an eye opener. So I was working at Woods, and I loved French Cuisine, but after going to Italy for a month tasting all the wonderful Italian Food and me being of Italian ancestry myself, I decided that I wanted to cook Italian. I needed to go and work with a great Italian Chef, and learn how to cook Italian. So I went looking for a new job. It would have to be at a great restaurant, with a great chef of good reputation. I went to Arqua, Sandro's, and Caio Bella. Well it turned out, all three chefs at all three places offered me a job. I chose Caio Bella which was a super hot Italian restaurant at the time. I worked with 3 Italian guys in that kitchen, Chef Pasquale, and Paulo and Stephano as well. I learn a lot there. I learned how to cook authentic Italian, and most important, *I learned how to make the perfect Bolognese.* And chef Pasquale showed me personally himself one day how to make it, and *I've been making the perfect Ragu Bolognese ever since.* I've become famous for my Bolognese, serving it to thousands of people, in both my personal life and in restaurants. Everyone just loves it, *my Bolognese is just so dam good* that I eventually became known as *Danny Bolognese.* The Journal of Italian Food Wine & Travel upon doing a six page article on me and my restaurant Bar Cichetti, went as far as to say that I made the *Best Bolognese in the America*, and the thousands of people I've cooked it for would agree. People that include; Bill Murray, Tony Bennett, Ed

Harris, Matt Dillon, and a whole string of celebrities I've cooked for over the years.

And yes many asked me for the recipe over the years. I've given the recipe to a very few close friends and family and taught a few how to make it personally. But I didn't want to publish my Secret Bolognese Recipe for a very long time. My Bolognese was a secret, and it remained so for years. A secret to all except for my cousins Joe, Joey Jr., and Edward, and my friends Pat P and Jimmy Starace, the very few who I taught to make this wonderful sauce by hand. But now my friends, it's time to let the cat out of the bag. So here it is, Danny's Famous Bolognese, the recipe that some say, "is the best in America." Enjoy!

BOLOGNESE a COOKBOOKELLA

Wow, this book is getting longer by the minute. When you write a book, you have an idea and concept, then your start to work it (write). So, originally this book was to be more or less about one of the greatest dishes the world has ever known, the Bolognese. It still is. The book was more or less conceived to finally bring my *famous Bolognese Sauce Recipe* to the World. And as I've said and I still maintain if I just wrote the Bolognese Recipe and sold it to people alone at this price and with no other recipes at all, then it would be more than worth it, *just for the Bolognese Recipe alone*. In fact just to get this Secret Bolognese Recipe alone and without any other recipes is a steal to you my dear reader or anyone else who buys this book. That's a fact. That is my belief, *some will agree*, some won't. Now in this day and age, with Kindle and other ebooks, many authors who write novels, are now because of the nature and being of things like Amazon, Kindle, iBooks and such, these novelist are taking to writing more novellas (short novels) and other smaller works, thus was my ideas for this little book called Bolognese. I would write a short book centered on Ragu Bolognese and my famous recipe for it. And though making available my famous secret Bolognese Recipe would be *worth the price of admission* alone, no, just like those guys on Television selling knives, blenders and what-not, I was going to throw in all sorts of other goodies. The goodies being more great Italian Recipes, besides the main attraction and *star of the show*, My Famous and Secret Recipe for Ragu Bolognese. So which recipes would they be? Well there wasn't going to be a ton of them, but this was the whole point. Make a book that's smaller-condensed and simplified, but with sixty-five or so of the most important and popular recipes of the entire Italian repertoire. So after the Bolognese, I think *Tomato Sauce,* that's the biggest and *most beloved dish of all,* and though everyone needs to know how to make a great one, not many do. So lets put in a recipe for perfect the Tomato Sauce and get things going. After that, you've just got to know how to make great Meatballs. OK, my Meatball Recipe goes in the book too. Everyone loves Lasagna! Yes lasagna goes in the book as well, and who doesn't need a great Cheesecake recipe? Everyone. So the book has grown. It's not one recipe, nor a full blown cookbook, shall we call it Cookbookella, as in a novella-length cookbook? Yes, I think this would be apropos. So here you go world, ladies and gentlemen, my little Cookbookella book on Ragu Bolognese and sixty or so of the most beloved Italian recipes of all. It's Bolognese, The Secret Recipe and more.

ABOUT THE BOLOGNESE

OK, the Bolognese? A Ragu Bolognese like most any other famous recipe as; the great French Cassoulet or Bouillabaisse, and the awesome Italian-American Sunday Gravy, there is no single one exact recipes. When it comes to Bolognese there are two areas that make for the greatest difference. The first is the meats to use. Some make their Bolognese with a mixture of Beef and Pork and with or without Pancetta, while some like myself and the late great Marcella Hazan make Bolognese with just the beef and no Pancetta. When Chef Pasquale taught me how to make the Bolognese that I've become famous for, he just used beef. So to this day beef is all I use, with no pork at all and no pancetta. You don't really need it. One thing that Pasquale showed me that not to many people put in their Bolognese, but yes some do, and which I always use, are dry Porcini Mushrooms. The mushrooms give the Bolognese a nice little extra depth of flavor, and you can either use them or not, and most actually don't, but that's the way Chef Pasquale showed me, and that's how I have always done it. No one has ever complained, believe me. I might add, that though not many people put dry Porcini Mushrooms in their Bolognese, the most esteemed Italian Chef in history, Chef Artusi Pellegrino who was the first person to publish (1891) a recipe for Ragu alla Bolognese put dry Porcini in his ragu. The recipe in Pellegrino's book is called Maccheroni alla Bolognese.

BOLOGNESE .. *The CLASSIC RECIPE*

This recipe for Ragu Bolognese is the one that is most classic. It's not my Bolognese, a.k.a. Danny's Bolognese, my recipe follows this one. They are both great recipes. As much as I love mine, this is equally as good and you can make it with or without the Pancetta. I recommend no Pancetta, but there are some who do use it, and it's up to you if you do so or not.

INGREDIENTS :

2 tablespoons olive oil
1 medium onion, minced
2 celery stalks & I carrot minced
2 pound ground Beef
1 pound ground Pork
3 ½ cups whole Milk
¼ teaspoon ground Nutmeg
3 cups Red Wine
2 - 28 ounce cans San Marzano Tomato Passata (puree)
5 tablespoons of Tomato Paste
3 cups water
3 tablespoons of sweet butter

PREPARATION :

Put olive oil and butter, celery, onion, and minced carrot in a large pot. Sauté over a low flame for 5 minutes. Add ground meats to the pot and cook until the meat has lost its raw color. Do not brown the meat or it will get hard. Break the meat up with a wooden spoon as you are cooking it.

Drain the fat off the meat mixture in a strainer. Put the drained meat back in the pot and season with Salt and Pepper.

Add milk and nutmeg and cook on low heat until the milk is reduced by half, about 8 minutes. Add wine and cook over high heat until the wine is reduced by half, about 6-7 minutes. Add tomatoes, tomato paste, and water.

Cook the sauce over the lowest flame possible for 3 to 3 ½ hours while stirring every few minutes to keep the sauce from burning.

Cook the pasta of your choice, Tagiatelle is the quintessential pasta for Bolognese, but you can also use Spaghetti, or a short maccheroni like Fusilli, Rigatoni, or Cavatappi.

Drain the cooked pasta in a colander. Put the pasta back in the pot it cooked in and mix it with some of the sauce and a knob of butter.

Plate the pasta onto each guest's plate and top with a little more of the Bolognese Sauce on top. Pass grated Grana Padano or Parmigiano Reggiano (do not serve with Pecorino Romano which is much to sharp for this Ragu). Enjoy your Bolognese.

NOTE : Make this recipe just as above, or if you want to add some Pancetta as some people do (I never do) you can add 4 ounces of minced Pancetta when you are cooking the vegetables.

DANNY'S BOLOGNESE
The Secret Recipe

OK, this is My Bolognese. It's the one that Chef Pasquale showed me how to make, way back in 1985. I taught my cousins Joe Macari and his sons Joey Jr. Tommy, and Eddie and my cousin Anthony Bellino how to make it. I also taught my friends my Pat P. and Jimmy Starace how to make it, and not many other people in this world until now. So here it is *Danny's Famous Bolognese.* It's a winner and I absolutely guarantee that it will more than please anyone and everyone you feed it to. There's absolutely no doubt about this. Sorry if I go on-and-on about it, but this is the affect the Bolognese has on one, *"it's that dam good!"* Learn how to make it properly and you're as good as gold. And here it is, *you lucky dog you*. I tell you, you are getting *the Bargain of the Century*, this recipe and all the others for just a few bucks. A steal I tell you. And I'm sure that you will agree, because once you learn how to make it (from this recipe), you will get years of enjoyment and fulfillment from it. You will nourish yourself, not just through your stomach, but in your mind, heart, and soul. You will see. I myself have always gotten a great amount of joy from making Bolognese and feeding it to others. Believe me my friends, making food and feeding it to those you love (or not) will always give you great joy.

I have done it for years and have countless memories of good times with many.

Making the Bolognese is oh so easy, once you have the right recipe (it's below). You make one big pot and you can feed a whole big group. It's nothing to feed 14 people or so at a dinner party. You make the Bolognese, get it simmering away, then you can prepare a simple antipasto or salad for the first course. You can make or buy some nice desserts or have one or your guests bring dessert.

You've got to have some good wine and good music (No Hip Hip or Heavy Metal please! Sinatra, Dean Martin, and Tony Bennett preferred) and you're going to have *the time of your life*, you've got Bolognese!

The BOLOGNESE ….

INGREDIENTS :

2 tablespoons olive oil
1 medium onion, minced
2 Celery Stalks & 1 Carrot minced
3 pounds Ground Beef
2 1/2 cups Red Wine
1 cup each water and chicken broth
2 - 28 ounce cans San Marzano Tomato Passata (puree)
5 tablespoons of Tomato Paste
2 oz. dried Porcini Mushrooms, soak in hot water 10 minutes to soften Mushrooms
2 sprigs each fresh Rosemary & Sage tied together w/ string
5 tablespoons of sweet butter
2 tablespoons Cream for each portion of pasta (optional)

PREPARATION :

Put olive oil and 2 tablespoons of butter with the celery, onion, and minced carrot in a large pot. Sauté over a low flame for five minutes.

Add ground meats to large pot and cook until the meat has lost its raw color. Do not brown the meat or it will get hard, some people do, but I don't recommend doing so. Break the meat up with a wooden spoon as you are cooking it.

Drain the fat off the meat mixture in a strainer. Put the drained meat back in the pot and season with Salt and Pepper.

Add wine and cook over high heat until the wine is reduced by half its original volume, about 5-6 minutes. Add tomato passata, tomato paste, dry Porcini Mushrooms, water, and chicken broth.

Cook the sauce over the lowest flame possible for 3 hours while stirring every few minutes to keep the sauce from burning. Add the Rosemary & Sage to the ragu after it has been cooking for 2 ½ hours.

After 3 hours simmering the Bolognese is now done. Remove the rosemary & sage from the pot and discard. Let the Bolognese rest while you cook your pasta. Tagiatelle (Fettuccine).

Cook the pasta according to directions on the package. Drain the cooked pasta in a colander, put it back in the pot it cooked in, add some Bolognese and a knob of butter to the pot and mix together.

Plate the pasta and add some more of the Bolognese on top of each plate of pasta. Serve with grated Parmigiano and Savor all of its goodness, it's Bolognese. And there's nothing better!

NOTE: When I was taught to make Bolognese by Chef Pasquale, he didn't put milk into the Bolognese, but just like the greatest Italian Chef of all-time Chef Artusi Pellegrino, he put a little cream into the Ragu Bolognese just before serving what Artusi called Maccheroni alla Bolognese. You can do it either way, serving the Bolognese with or without a little cream (2 tablespoons for each serving). The cream helps give a little more extra rich flavor and smooth texture at the end.
I myself make the Bolognese without the milk and then depending on my whim each time I serve it, I either put a little cream in at the end or not. You add a little knob of butter when mixing the pasta with the Ragu, and by adding Parmigano Reggiano grated over the top of the pasta this gives the Bolognese the same creamy richness as when using cream or milk.

If Using The Cream :

Once you have your pot of Ragu Bolognese simmering on the top of the stove, add 2 tablespoons of Heavy Cream to the Ragu for each person you will be serving and let the cream simmer in with the Ragu for 8 to 10 minutes. Cook your pasta and serve with the Bolognese. You now in 7th Heaven, Enjoy!

NOTE II : As we've said, Tagiatelle pasta is most traditional, but Spaghetti or some short maccheroni are great as well, it's up to you, you choose the pasta.

PASTA ANTIPASTO and More !!!

This is not your typical cookbook, or Italian-Cookbook for that matter. Most Italian Cookbooks start with Antipasto items, then soup and pasta, then Fish, Meat & Poultry, and finishing up with desserts. This cookbook is special and the main focus is of my famous Secret Ragu Bolognese, the dish, the *Recipe*. At the price of this book, it would be worth it just for my Secret Bolognese Sauce *alone, f*or once you know how to make this famous Bolognese, you'll be a God. You'll be revered by friends and family simply because you can make this one great dish, The Bolognese. It's that good!

But hey, I couldn't write a cookbook and put just one recipe in it, no matter how wonderful, even though it might quite possibly be, *the one single greatest dish ever*. No, that just wouldn't be right. I thought about how to put this all together, and what other recipes to include. Well what I came up with, is, make a nice small condensed cookbook of the best and most popular Italian-American dishes of all, including the greatest dish of all, Ragu alla Bolognese. Include recipes for dishes that are so tasty and great that people eat them over and over and never get tired of them, but relish these dishes each and every time, and that's why they're so great, people just can't get enough of them.
So what are they? Well besides the great and wonderful Bolognese, you've got to have Tomato

Sauce, the backbone of all Italian Cooking. Right? Yes, of course. And who doesn't love *Lasagna*? No one I tell you. So we've included it as well. Also, I've included a few of the most important Antipasti items and Salad because once you know how to make this famous Bolognese, and you want to have a dinner party for your friends, you're gonna need something to start with. So you've got a couple antipasto items or salad to proceed the *great Bolognese.* And as I love to cook for friends and family, but mostly just savory food and not sweets. So when I cook for friends, I have one of the guest bring some desserts, or I'll pick up some pastry or other dessert at the bakery, and that's that. But although I usually don't cook sweets any more (I used to) I know that some do. And who doesn't love Italian Cheesecake and needs a recipe for one? So it's in here. Remember I said I used to cook sweets, and I used to be famous for my Cheesecake, so I've included it n here. It's at the end of the book, and that's all you need.

So yes, I've said this is not your normal cookbook but a special one, and one that is centered around one of the World's great dishes, if not the *Greatest of All*, yes the Ragu Bolognese. So instead of starting with Antipasto and Salads, the Bolognese is first and foremost, Front & Center and everything else follows after it. Hey, I'm giving you my Bolognese, and everything else is an extra special added treat, or as we say "it's *Gravy!"*

INSALATA CAPRESE
... Tomato Mozzarella Salad

This salad is the easiest thing in the world to make, with the hardest part being to find perfect ripe tomatoes to complement the fresh mozzarella and basil. Once you find good fresh ripe tomatoes, and you've got your Mozzarella & Basil, all you have to do is slice the tomatoes and mozzarella and dress all with a little salt & pepper, the basil, and good quality Italian Olive Oil and you're all set. Put on some nice Italian Music, get a nice bottle of white or red wine (Greco di Tufo or Aglianico) that comes from the region and you're all set. Pretend you're on Capri and you're in Heaven.

INGREDIENTS :

1 pound Fresh Mozzarella
3-4 ripe Salad Tomatoes (washed)
8 fresh Basil Leaves (washed & dried)
3 tablespoons Italian Olive Oil
Sea Salt & Black Pepper

Slice the Mozzarella into 8 equal slices.

Place the Basil leaves one-on-top-of-the other. Roll them up. Slice the roll of basil leaves to get thin slices of Basil.

Put half the olive oil onto a plate. Slice the tomatoes into 12 equal slices. Place the tomato slices down on the plate of olive to coat each tomato slice with olive oil. Turn each slice over. Sprinkle a little salt and black pepper over each slice of tomato. Evenly distribute the Basil over all 12 slices of tomato.

Get 4 clean plates that you will be serving the Caprese Salad on.

Place one slice of tomato down on the plate. Then lay one slice of mozzarella halfway over the tomato slice. Add another slice of tomato to go halfway over the 1st slice of mozzarella, then place another slice of mozzarella halfway over the 2nd slice of tomato. Place a 3rd and final slice of tomato over the 2nd slice of mozzarella. Repeat this process until you have four plates of Caprese Salad of equal portions. Serve to your guests and enjoy.

HOW to MAKE an ITALIAN SALAD

How to make an Italian Salad? Good question. Well as they say, *there's more than one way to skin a cat*, and when it comes to making salads, and Italian Salads in particular, this is oh so true. First off there are two main ways, and from these two there are all sorts of variations on the theme. First off, the most basic and really true Italian Salad is made by getting the best lettuce of your choice and some nice ripe tomatoes. You wash and dry both the lettuce and tomatoes, then place them in a large glass or ceramic mixing bowl. Then all you do is drizzle in a little Italian Olive Oil and mix. You then season with a little Kosher or Sea Salt and ground Black Pepper and mix again. You then put in a little vinegar and mix, and Voila, your salad is set and ready to go. So that's how Italian's for many years made their salads. The French, Americans and most others do it a little differently. They make the dressing in a small bowl (or buy Ready Made), put the lettuce and whatever other ingredients they have for the salad in a large bowl, add the ready made dressing, and mix. Please note and keep in mind that the standard universal proportions of Vinegar to Oil for salad dressings is 3 parts Oil to 1 part Vinegar. The Italians on the other had like and put a bit more vinegar on their salads, at about 35% vinegar to 65% Olive Oil, whereas the French and others use 25% Vinegar to 75% or 3 to 1 .. You can do whichever way you like, it's all up to your liking and preferences.

RECIPE : A BASIC ITALIAN SALAD

1 head Boston Bibb Lettuce (washed and dried)
2 medium sized ripe Salad Tomatoes (washed)
1 Cucumber, peeled and sliced
9 tablespoons good quality Italian Olive Oil
3 – 4 tablespoons good quality Italian Red Wine Vinegar
½ teaspoon Kosher or Sea Salt
½ teaspoon ground Black Pepper

Break up lettuce leaves and place in a large glass or ceramic bowl.

Slice the Cucumber in-half along the length, the slice each half into thin slices. Place Cucumber slices in the bowl with lettuce and mix.

Add Olive Oil to bowl and mix. Add salt & pepper and mix gently. Add vinegar and mix.

Plate the salad among in four equal portions on 4 plates.

Cut the tomatoes in half, the cut each half into equal size wedges.

Place the tomatoes in the bowl that you mixed the salad in. Season the tomatoes with a little salt & Black Pepper and mix. You can add a bit more olive oil if you feel you need it. Arrange the tomatoes nicely on the plates with the salad and serve.

Note: You can use whatever lettuce you like besides the Boston Bibb (Meslcum, Romaine, etc.). Also a nice little touch is to add a ½ teaspoon of dry Oregano to tomatoes when seasoning (optional).

ITALIAN SALAD DRESSING

RECIPE:

2/3 cup Italian Olive Oil
¼ cup Italian Red Wine Vinegar (Best Quality)
½ teaspoon of Kosher or Sicilian Sea Salt
1 teaspoon dry Oregano
½ teaspoon dry Basil
2 cloves Garlic, peeled and minced (optional)
2 tablespoons Dijon Mustard (optional)

To make this salad dressing. If you have a nice small empty re-sealable glass jar, put all the ingredients in the glass jar or other container and shake vigorously. That's it you're done.

If you don't won't to make it this way, then place all ingredients in a small bowl and whisk ingredients together with a wire-whip. You're done.

Once your dressing is made, get whatever lettuce you like; Iceberg, Mesclum, Romaine, whatever? You can simply have the salad with just lettuce, or do as most Italian-Americans do and add Cucumbers & Tomatoes to your salad. You can even add some cheese, which is real nice. Suitable cheese would be, Gorgonzola or other Blue Cheese, Mozzarella, or shave Parmesan.

SHRIMP COCKTAIL

Shrimp Cocktail is a great favorite of just about all Italians, and all of America for that matter. Originally not really Italian, but Italian-Americans have adopted it into their cuisine. Once Upon a Time, Shrimp Cocktail was on just about every Italian Restaurant Menu in America.

HOW to MAKE IT :

2 lbs. Large Shrimp, cleaned
1 tablespoon of Salt, ½ cup Tomato Ketchup
3 tablespoons Prepared Horseradish
8 drops Tabasco sauce or other Hot Sauce Brand

Bring a large pot of salted water to the boil.

Add shrimp. Bring back to the boil and once the water comes back to the boil, lower heat to lowest flame and cook for about 4-5 minutes until shrimp are cooked through and you do not see any rawness in the center.

Immediately remove from heat, and drain water off shrimp. Add shrimp to a large bowl of water with ice to stop the cooking. Let sit for 5 minutes. Drain the shrimp of all water and set to the side.

In a small glass or ceramic bowl, mix the horseradish, Ketchup and Hot Sauce. This is the Cocktail Sauce for the shrimp. Neatly arrange shrimp on a plate or platter over some Bibb Lettuce and serve with the cocktail sauce in a small bowl.

ANTIPASTO MISTI

The iconic Mixed Antipasto of the Italian-American table is ubiquitous. Once upon a time you could find it on almost every Italian restaurant menu in America, not so much anymore. Yes the mixed antipasto is ubiquitous, but usually anything that is known in this manner, it's for a reason. The reason being that the thing whatever it may be is great and wonderful and every loves it, thus it becomes universal, is seen everywhere and all the time (almost) that it becomes what? Ubiquitous, which has at times become a dirty word. Well not dirty, but for sure, not always complimentary. Never-the-less, the Antipasto as we call it is great. It's much loved, and although it's not found on as many Italian restaurant menus anymore, any good old old-school Italian joints that are still around, they'll surely have it. It's ubiquitous, but it's great, and people love it, and when it comes to Italian-Americans in their homes and having a Sunday dinner when the whole family gathers round, guess what? For the first course, it's a good chance you'll find an Antipasto on the table. We still love it.

So, the Mixed Antipasto, what's on it? Well, most times you'll be able to guess the ingredients. You'll almost always have some sort of Salumi, with Cheese, and some kind of vegetables, like Roast Peppers and fresh Celery Sticks or Giardiniera (Pickled Italian Vegetables), or marinated Artichoke Hearts.

For those who may not know, when we say Salumi, the word Salumi means all cured Italian meats, mostly made of pork. Salami is one type of Salumi products. In America most often Genoa Salami most popular around the country, but we in New York prefer Sopresseta, either sweet or hot.

To make a nice easy Antipasto that has a good variety that everyone will love, get some good Sweet Sopresseta, Provolone Cheese, a jar of good quality Roast Red Peppers, some large Green Sicilian Olives and maybe some fresh Celery Sticks. This is your basic mixed antipasto that many Italian-American families would make. If you make one like this, you'll be doing very well. If you like you can add more to this basic antipasto with one or more of the following items; Fresh Mozzarella, Prosciutto, Mortadella, Capicola (Gabagool), a jar of marinated Artichoke Hearts, and or Eggplant Caponata.

Make some sort of mixed antipasto as described above and you will be having a wonderful beginning of a great and memorable Bolognese dinner. Yes, serve a mixed antipasto preceding your wonderful Pasta Bolognese or whatever your main course you're having. Get some good Italian Wine and maybe a little dessert and you're sure to have a hit dinner party on your hands. Also, if you want to throw an easy no fuss little Wine & Antipasto Party instead of a Wine & Cheese Party, make a nice Antipasto that has a good variety of meats (Salumi), cheese, and vegetable items like; Olives, Caponata, and Artichoke Hearts, your gonna have a winner of a party on your hands. And you hardly have to do any work to do something like this, there's no cooking, only buying some wonderful already made products that are of the highest quality. Do this and enjoy, your friends will love it.

ASPARAGUS PARMIGIANO

Asparagus Parmigiano is one of the easiest and tastiest antipasto items of all, and quite healthy to boot. This dish can be served as either an antipasto item on its own, as a vegetable side dish (Contorno) or with one or two fried eggs on top in the form of Asparagi Milanese, eaten as a light lunch or dinner.

The first time I ever made this dish for my cousins at a family meal we were having, all my cousins went nuts for it. None of them had ever had it before, and they were all astonished at how tasty it was, and the ease, quickness, and simplicity of preparation, they couldn't believe it. After they all had it, they all asked me to tell them how to make it, I told them the simple steps involved and now they all make this dish at their own homes all the time. And now you can make it too. And remember, you can serve it as an antipasto, side dish, or a light main-course meal with 1 or 2 fried eggs on top. It's as easy as pie!

INGREDIENTS :

20-24 medium stalks Asparagus
1/3 cup grated Parmigiano Reggiano or Grana Padano Cheese
2 ½ tablespoons Butter
2 tablespoons of Olive Oil
Salt

Cut off woody bottom ends of the Asparagus. Gently peel off bottom half of each Asparagus stalk, being careful not to peel off more than the skin and not the meat of the asparagus.

In a small pan, melt butter on low heat. Turn heat off once butter is melted and set the butter aside.

Put on a large pot of boiling salted water to cook the asparagus in. Turn oven on to 400 degrees.

Place the cleaned asparagus in the boiling salted water. Cook the asparagus for 3 minutes. Quickly remove asparagus from water and place in a colander or large wire strainer.

Coat a cookie sheet pan with the olive oil. Place asparagus in four equal portions next to each other on the cookie pan. If you have 20 asparagus you will make4 groups of 5 asparagus each, and if you have 24, you will make four groups of six asparagus side-by-side.

Evenly pour the melted butter over all the asparagus. Top all the asparagus evenly with the grated cheese.

Bake asparagus in 400 degree oven for 7 minutes. Remove asparagus from oven and plate equal portions on 4 plates and serve.

Danny Bolognese

APSPARAGUS MILANESE

To make Asparagus Milanese, first make Asparagus Parmigiano, then top each portion of Asparagus Parmigiano with 1 or 2 Fried Eggs each and you're all set, you've made Asparagus Milanese, and you're gonna be amazed at how good it is. Mangia Bene!

STUFFED ZUCCHINI

Stuffed Zucchini makes quite a nice Hot Antipasto item. Serve one for an antipasto or two along with a little Mixed Green Salad or a nice tasty light lunch.

INGREDIENTS :

6 medium sized Zucchini, washed
¼ cup Olive Oil
1 small Onion, peeled and minced fine
1 clove Garlic, peeled and minced
½ cup Button Mushrooms chopped fine
½ cup plain Breadcrumbs
½ teaspoon Salt
½ teaspoon ground Black Pepper
½ teaspoon Paprika
¼ cup Milk
¼ cup grated Parmigiano Reggiano or Grana Padano
¼ cup fresh chopped Italian Parsley

Cut the zucchini in half down the length of the each zucchini.

Scoop out the pulp of the zucchini making little boats out of each zucchini. Carefully slice a small sliver of skin off the opposite side of each Zucchini Boat, being careful not to cut too much or make a hole in the zucchini.

Place the zucchini bottom side down a baking dish coated with a little olive oil, and cook in a 350 degree for 10 minutes.

Cook the onion, Mushrooms, and garlic together on low heat until all cooked through, about 8-10 minutes. As you are cooking mushrooms and onions, season with a little salt and pepper and stir as you cook. When finished cooking, remove from heat and set in aside in a mixing bowl to cool for 15 minutes.

Once the mushroom mixture has cooled, add the grated cheese, breadcrumbs, and most of the Parsley to the bowl and mix.

Stuff the Zucchini Boats with the Mushroom Stuffing.

Place the stuffed Zucchini Barquettes on the oiled baking pan and cook in a 360 degree oven for 16 minutes.

Serve one piece of Stuffed Zucchini sprinkled with a little chopped Parsley to each one of your guests.

ZUCCHINI PIE

INGREDIENTS :

4 medium Zucchini
1 small Red Bell Pepper, seeded and sliced
1 small Onion, peeled and sliced
1 ¼ cups plain Breadcrumbs
1 ½ cups grated Parmigiano Reggiano
¼ cup Olive Oil
Salt & Black Pepper to taste
½ pound Mozzarella Cheese, cut into 1 ½ " cubes
1 Egg
¼ fresh chopped Italian Parsley

Place 8 tablespoons of Olive Oil in a large pan with the Red Bell Pepper and cook on medium heat for 8 minutes. Add the onions to pan, season with Salt & Black Pepper and cook on low heat for 8 minutes. Remove Peppers and Onions and set aside

Cook the Zucchini in two separate batches in the pan. Cook on medium heat until the zucchini are slightly brown on both sides. Season with a few pinches of Salt & Pepper. Place in a glass bowl and let sit.

Place the breadcrumbs in a small bowl with 1/3 of the grated Parmigiano. Add the Parsley, 5 tablespoons of water, and 6 tablespoons of Olive Oil and mix.

Beat the egg and pour into the bowl with the zucchini. Add 1/3 the remaining grated Parmigiano and mix.

Get a 9" glass Pie Pan (or metal) and coat the bottom with a film of olive oil. Place half the Peppers & Onion mixture on the bottom of the pan. Sprinkle with a little of the grated cheese, then lay half of the Zucchini over this and top the zucchini with half of the diced Mozzarella.

Place remaining Zucchini in the pan, then top with the remaining Mozzarella. Sprinkle all of the Breadcrumbs on top of the pie and bake in a 350 degree oven for 18 minutes.

Remove from oven and serve as an antipasto course or side-dish on the side of any; chicken, fish, or meat dinner.

The Zucchini Pie also makes a nice little light lunch, accompanied with a small Green Salad on the side. Enjoy.

PICKLED STRING BEANS
Fagiolini Raccolti alla Nonna

These Pickled String Beans are great to make ahead of time and leave in your cupboard to serve anytime at a moments notice. My grandmother always had these Picked Beans on hand at all times, along with her Pickled Eggplant and Roast Peppers. Having these items on hand, if unexpected company came over, she could layout a beautiful Antipasto Misto on the table in a few minutes flat. You could serve these wonderful Pickled Green Beans on their own as an antipasto, or couple with Salami, Provolone, and or nice ripe in-season sliced tomatoes, and you're already to go.

INGREDIENTS :

3 pounds String Beans
2 medium Red Onions, peeled and sliced fine
3 cloves Garlic, peeled and left whole
¾ cup Olive Oil
1 cup Italian Red Wine Vinegar
1 tablespoon Kosher or Sea Salt
1 teaspoon ground Black Pepper
½ teaspoon Red Pepper Flakes
1 Bay Leaf

Wash the String Beans and cut off the end tips.

Cook string beans in a large amount of boiling salted water until just slightly tender, yet still firm and crisp, about 3-4 minutes at most.

Quickly remove from heat and drain in a colander. Put the beans back in the pot they cooked in and run cold water over the beans for 8 minutes to cool well.

Drain the Green Beans again in the colander and shake off all excess water.

Mix all remaining ingredients in a large bowl.

Fill large 1 quart Mason Jars with the String Beans. Then fill the jars with the Vinegar Mixture to top of jar. Seal Jars and store in the refrigerator for at least one day before serving.

These Pickled Beans will keep for months, but they'll probably be gone in 10 days or less, cause they so good and very handy to have around. Enjoy.

DANNY'S BASLAMIC WINGS

Here's a dish I created that stems from some other chicken wings that I'm famous for, My Famous Honey Mustard Chicken Wings. Well I switched some Baslamic Vinegar Glaze for the some of the Honey to give the wings and Italian spin, and here we go, Danny's Famous Baslamic Chicken Wings, they're tasty as heck, I'm sure you'll agree.

INGREDIENTS :

2 pounds Chicken Wings, tip removed and Wings cut in half
9 tablespoons Olive Oil
½ teaspoon Kosher Salt
¼ teaspoon each of Black Pepper and Hot Red Pepper Flakes
3 tablespoons Soy Sauce
10 tablespoons Baslamic Vinegar
6 tablespoons Honey
8 tablespoons Baslamic Vinegar Glaze

Turn oven on to 400 degrees. Place the Chicken Wings in a large baking pan with the Olive Oil, Salt, and Black Pepper and mix so the chicken is completely coated with the Salt, Pepper, and oil.

Place in the oven and let roast at 400 degrees for 10 minutes. Take out of oven and place 10 tablespoons Baslamic Vinegar and the Soy Sauce in the pan and mix with the Chicken.

Put the Chicken back in the oven and let roast at 350 degrees for 15 minutes.

Take Chicken out of the oven and put the Baslamic Vinegar Glaze, the Honey, and Red Pepper in the pan and mix. Put back in the oven and roast at 325 degrees for 6 minutes. Remove chicken from oven.

Mix the chicken and sauce once again, then et Chicken rest for 7 minutes before serving, and enjoy.

TOMATO SAUCE

Tomato Sauce? It's the backbone of all Italian cooking. The sauce is used everywhere, on Pizza, in Eggplant Parmigiano, on Veal Parms, with Pasta & Zucchini or Cucuzza, all over the place. And as much as we love Bolognese, when it comes to importance and the single one most popular Italian Sauce of all, nothing beats Tomato Sauce, aka Salsa Pomodoro. Tomato Sauce is the absolute undisputed champ of the Italian Kitchen. And if you don't know how to make a good Tomato Sauce, then you don't know how to cook Italian. Here's a great recipe, of which you'll be astonished how easy it is to make. But easiness and simplicity is what it's all about when it comes to Italian Cooking and making a correct Salsa Pomodoro (Tomato Sauce). The thing is, as simply as it is, there's a right way and a wrong way, and tomato sauce must be done right. The recipe is below, so dig in, and good luck.

TOMATO SAUCE … The RECIPE

INGREDIENTS:

3 - 28 ounce cans San Marzano Tomato Passata
or other good quality tomatoes
7 cloves minced garlic, 1 small onion minced
½ teaspoon crushed red pepper
¼ cup virgin olive oil, ¼ cup chopped fresh Basil
Salt and pepper to taste

In a 6 quart or larger pot, sauté onions over a low flame for 3 minutes. Add garlic and cook for 3-4 minutes. Do not let the garlic get dark or burn.

Add tomatoes, turn heat up to high and stir. When sauce starts to bubble, turn flame down so the sauce is at a low simmer. Simmer for 45 minutes while frequently stirring the bottom of the pan to keep sauce from burning. Add fresh basil in the last ten minutes of cooking.

Cook whatever pasta you choose according to directions on package, spaghetti is best. When the pasta is finished cooking, drain in a colander. Put pasta back in the pot it cooked in with a few tablespoons of reserved pasta cooking water. Add some sauce and a little olive oil and mix. Plate the pasta and top with a little more sauce on top. Serve to guest and pass around grated cheese.

MARINARA

Marinara Sauce is widely used in Italian-American Cuisine, and the sauce can vary from person to person and, cook-to-cook, chef-to-chef, restaurant to restaurant, "there is no one single exacting specific recipe, but all usually have Olive Oil, Garlic, Tomato, Pepperoncino, and Basil and or Oregano. Oregano seems to be the biggest single factor in what a Marinara Sauce actually is, as many versions of Marinara Sauce seem to have Oregano included in it, which is not usually present in true Italian (of and from Italy) Tomato Sauce, or Sugo al Pomodoro. One other factor, is that Marinara Sauce is cooked quickly, in about 18 minutes as opposed to 45 minutes or longer for regular Tomato Sauce.

OK, now, my Marinara Sauce, what I think it is, and how I make it. It's also how, not everyone but many others make it as well. Remember, I am of Italian-American heritage, and I cooked professionally for 20 years in French, then Italian-Restaurants. To me, the way I was taught and what I think is the best tasting Marinara Sauce and what most think of as Marinara is as follows. To make Marinara Sauce, I already have my base regular Tomato Sauce that I have made previously. When I was in a restaurant and someone wanted Marinara Sauce, this is the one we made. We'd use about a cup and a 1/2 of our regular tomato sauce that was always on hand. When we got an order for

Spaghetti Marinara, we'd put some Olive Oil and a single serving pan. Heat it, add a good amount of chopped fresh Garlic. Cook the garlic and a bit of Pepperoncino (Red Pepper Flakes) and a little dried Oregano. This was our flavoring base, and it would considerably add much flavor to the base Tomato Sauce, making for a quite tasty Marinara. Once the garlic has cooked to where it just starts to brown a bit, you add the Tomato Sauce and heat through. Once your spaghetti has finished cooking, you drain it, drop it in the pan with your Marinara Sauce, adding a bit of the pasta cooking water, toss the pasta (mix) and serve. Voila, Spaghetti Marinara, my version and the one most accepted as Marinara in professional Italian kitchens in New York, the most respected in all of America. This is not the defining Marinara Sauce Recipe, but I believe the one most widely used, certainly in restaurants in New York. And no matter, I can tell you it's dam tasty and, I always get raves whenever I make it.

So in the end, what is marinara? As I've said there is no one right singular answer, or description. But if you ask me and most any renowned Italian-American home cook or professional New York cooks and chefs, this is the Marinara most acknowledged.

MARINARA SAUCE RECIPE

NOTE: To make this Marinara Sauce, you first have to make the previous recipe Tomato Sauce. This proportion of Sauce is for 4 people of which you will cook 1 pound of Spaghetti or other dry Pasta. Dry pasta is best for tomato sauce, not fresh unless you use Gnocchi or Ravioli. As you will see by making this Marinara Sauce, what marinara is basically a flavored tomato sauce (our version of Marinara). You are taking some Tomato Sauce that has already been made, then flavoring it with a good amount of Garlic in Olive Oil with Red Pepper Flakes (not too much), and if you like some dry Oregano. Try it, you'll not like it, but Love It! Basta!

Ingredients:

6 cup Home-Made Tomato Sauce
6 tablespoons olive oil
7 cloves Garlic, peeled and chopped fine
Pepperoncino (Red Pepper flakes), 1/8 of a teaspoon
Oregano is "Optional" ¼ to ½ teaspoon if you use it

Heat olive oil with garlic over medium flame for 2 minutes.

Add Pepperoncino and Oregano if you are using it and cook 1 minute. Add homemade Sugo di Pomodoro (Tomato Sauce) that you cooked previously. Cook over medium heat for 3-4 minutes and you've got Marinara Sauce.

SPAGHETTI PUTTANESCA

Legend has it that this pasta dish was made by Neapolitan Ladies of the evening, who would whip up this dish real fast in-between customers. Some accounts have restaurateur Sandro Petti inventing it at his trattoria on the Island of Ischia in the Bay of Naples late one evening to serve to some late-night diners when no other ingredients were available but the ones in this pasta, so he threw them together and might have made what was the first Spaghetti Puttanesca back in the 1950's. Who knows? No matter who invented it the dish is bold in flavor and loved by millions.

INGREDIENTS :

¼ cup Olive Oil
5 Anchovy Filets minced fine
6 cloves Garlic, peeled and minced
¼ large Green Olives, chopped (Pits removed)
¼ cup Black Olives, chopped (Pits removed)
¼ Capers
5 – 6 cups Tomato Sauce (from recipe in book)
¼ cup fresh chopped Italian Parsley
1 pound imported Italian Spaghetti

Put on a large pot of boiling salted water.

Place the Garlic, Anchovies, and Olive Oil in a large frying pan. Cook on medium heat for 4 minutes. Add all remaining ingredients except the Parsley and cook on low heat for 12 minutes while you cook the pasta.

Cook the spaghetti according to directions on package. Drain the spaghetti in a colander, reserving about ¼ cup of the cooking water. Place the pasta back into the pot it cooked in and add half the sauce and half the parsley. Mix together well.

Plate the Spaghetti onto four plates and divide remaining sauce equally over the top of the 4 plates of pasta. Sprinkle each plate with a little of the chopped Parsley and serve. Buon Appetito!

SPAGHETTI al PESTO

Here is a dish that should be in any serious Italian Cooks arsenal of recipes. Pasta with Pesto is one of the most classic of all Italian dishes and is wonderful in the famed vegetable soup Minestrone alla Genovese.

Pesto is a famous sauce from the Ligurian Coast of Italy, other-wise known as the Italian Riviera. The capital city is the port of Genoa. Pesto in Italy is only served on pasta in Italy, but many Americans who love this tasty sauce put it on everything from Chicken to Fish and more. It actually is great on a simple grilled or roast piece of fish or grilled chicken, so make a batch and keep in the refrigerator for whatever you like.

INGREDIENTS :

2 fresh bunches of Basil (about 6 ounces)
2 cloves Garlic, peeled
¼ cup best quality Italian Olive Oil
5 tablespoons Pignoli (Pine Nuts)
¼ teaspoon Salt

½ cup grated Parmigiano Reggiano or Grana Padano
1 pound imported Spaghetti, Linguine or any pasta you choose

Place the Basil, Pine Nuts, and garlic in a blender with half the olive oil and blend on high speed until all ingredients are completely blended, about 2 minutes.

Add remaining olive oil a little at a time until it is all incorporated.

Remove the pesto from the blender and place in a ceramic or glass bowl. Add the grated Parmigiano and salt and mix with a spoon.

Cook the pasta according to directions on package in a large pot of boiling salted water.

Drain the pasta in a colander, reserving a few tablespoons of water. Add reserved water and the pasta back into the pot it cooked in. Add a third of a cup of pesto sauce to pot and mix with the pasta and reserved pasta water.

Plate the Spaghetti Pesto onto four plates and top each pasta with some more of the Pesto Sauce and serve.

SPAGHETTI AMATRICIANA

In the pantheon of Italian cooking, Amatriciana is one of the most important Pasta Sauces of all. Basically, Amatriciana is a tomato sauce that is flavored with either Guiancale or Pancetta (Italian Bacon). The act of cooking the pork product (Pancetta or other) in the tomato sauce makes for an absolutely fabulous sauce., and topped with some grated cheese, you'll be in 7th *Heaven* eating it.

Like the Bolognese, I learned this recipe from chef Pasquale, and he taught me how to make it with a combination of Italian Pancetta and Smoked Bacon. This is not the norm, but making it this way. I've actually had Italians from Italy after eating my Amatriciana at my restaurant Bar Cichetti tell me that it was the *best* Amatriciana they'd ever had. "Seriously, no lie." That's a fact, and this is the highest complement one could ever get, for one thing about Italians from Italy, when it comes to food they do not pull any punches. If they don't like the taste of something, they'll let you know. Believe me, it's so true, those Italian guys love my Amatriciana so much, they came back to eat it again the next night. This is all you need to know about my awesome Amatriciana. Basta!

INGREDIENTS:

3 medium onions, sliced thinly. ¼ cup olive oil
1 teaspoon crushed Red Pepper flakes
1 lb. smoked bacon and ½ lb. pancetta diced
2-28 oz. cans crushed tomatoes
3 cloves garlic, minced
kosher or sea salt and black pepper to taste
1 & 1/2 lbs. imported Italian Spaghetti, Bucatini or other pasta

Place bacon and pancetta in a large frying pan and cook over very low heat to render fat (about 12 minutes). Do not brown or let bacon get hard or crispy.

Remove bacon and pancetta from pan and set aside. Drain all but 3 tablespoons of fat from pan. Add olive oil and onions to pan and sauté over low heat for about 12 minutes. Add garlic and red pepper, sauté for three minutes.

Add tomatoes, bacon, and pancetta. Simmer for 40 minutes.

Cook Bucatini or other pasta. Drain pasta, sprinkle with olive oil. Add sauce, mix and plate. Serve with grated Parmigiano.

Ragu Bolognese Cookbook

PASTA w/ MUSHROOM SAUCES Plus Two

This is a great Italian-American favorite that used be quite a bit more popular in days gone by than it is now. This said, it's still wonderful and many still like it to this day. The dish is easy to make, tasty, and soul satisfying. One great thing about knowing how to make this dish, is that once you know how to make Pasta with Mushroom Sauce, you will then know how to make several other dishes, simply by switching out the mushrooms for another ingredient like Zucchini or Cucuzza to make Pasta w/ Zucchini or the Sicilian-American favorite Pasta Gagootz! Can you beat that, 3 or more recipe in one? E' Buono!

RECIPE :

1 - 28 ounce can Tomato Passata or crushed tomatoes
3 cloves minced garlic
1 small onion, minced
½ teaspoon crushed red pepper
10 tablespoons olive oil
¼ cup chopped fresh Basil
Salt and pepper to taste
2 tablespoons Butter (optional)
12 ounces Button Mushrooms, or any mushrooms you like

Wash mushrooms, fry them off, then slice them.

In a 6 quart or larger pot, sauté onions over a low flame for 3 minutes. Add garlic and cook for 3-4 minutes. Do not let the garlic get dark or burn.

Add mushrooms and butter to the pot with onions and garlic and cook on medium heat until the mushrooms get a light golden color throughout, about 8 minutes.

Add tomatoes to pot, turn heat up to high and stir. When sauce starts to bubble, turn flame down so the sauce is at a low simmer. Simmer for 45 minutes while frequently stirring the bottom of the pan to keep sauce from burning. Add fresh basil in the last ten minutes of cooking.

Cook whatever pasta you choose according to directions on package. Spaghetti or Rigatoni work best. When the pasta is finished cooking, drain in a colander. Put pasta back in the pot it cooked in with a few tablespoons of reserved pasta cooking water. Add some sauce and a little olive oil and mix. Plate the pasta and top with a little more sauce on top. Serve to guest and pass around grated cheese.

For MUSHROOMS SAUCE without TOMATO:

If you like, you can also make a Mushroom Sauce without any tomato at all. If you do so, you're better off with some type of mushroom like; Shitakes, Crimini, and or Portobello Mushrooms. Just get double the amount of mushrooms and garlic, clean and slice them and sauté them in just olive oil and garlic or in a combination of Olive Oil with Butter and Garlic. You'll want to get a bit of fresh chopped Italian Parsley to through in at the end for both color and fresh taste. So cook the mushrooms until golden brown. Cook the pasta, drain it then toss the pasta with the mushrooms and parsley and serve.

For MUSHROOM CREAM SAUCE :

To make a Mushroom Cream Sauce, do the same as above recipe, but don't use any olive oil but butter instead to cook the mushrooms. Use less or no garlic, but still use parsley. Once the mushrooms are golden brown, add ½ a cup of heavy cream, season with salt & pepper and cook on medium heat until the cream has reduced by half, about 6 - 7 minutes. Turn heat off and add parsley and 1/3 cup of grated Parmigiano Reggiano Cheese and mix. Cook pasta, drain, the toss with sauce and serve.

Ragu Bolognese Cookbook

FUSILLI alla SICILIANA

The RECIPE :

2 - 28 ounce cans crushed Tomatoes
2 medium Zucchini, washed and sliced
1 medium Onion, peeled and rough chopped
7 cloves minced garlic
2 Sweet Red Bell Peppers, washed
1 small onion, minced
½ teaspoon crushed red pepper
¼ cup virgin olive oil
¼ cup chopped fresh Basil
Salt and pepper to taste
¼ cup large Sicilian Green Olives, pits removed
8 tablespoons Sicilian or other Capers
1 pound Italian Fusilli or other pasta (serves 4)

Cut the red peppers in half. Remove seeds and inner pith. Cut halves of peppers into ¼" slices. Slice the Zucchini.

Add olive oil and Red Bell Peppers to pot and cook on low heat for 12 minutes.

Add Zucchini and onions and cook on low heat for 6 minutes. Add garlic and continue cooking on low heat for 3 minutes.

Add tomatoes, turn heat up to high and stir. When sauce starts to bubble, turn flame down so the sauce is at a low simmer.

Simmer for 25 minutes while frequently stirring the bottom of the pan to keep sauce from burning. Add fresh basil the Olives & Capers and cook 5 minutes more.

You can serve this sauce with whatever pasta you choose. Cook pasta according to directions on package.

When the pasta is finished cooking, drain it in a colander, the put the pasta back in the pot it cooked in with a few tablespoons of reserved pasta cooking water. Add some sauce and a little olive oil and mix. Plate the pasta and top with a little more sauce on top. Serve to guest and pass around grated cheese.

NOTE : This is enough sauce for 8 to 10 servings. One pound of pasta is enough for 4 people. If you're feeding 6 to 8 people, cook 2 pounds of pasta, and this will be enough sauce. Enjoy.

LASAGNA

Lasagna, everyone loves it! Of course we do, we're Italian-American! But not only us, but all Americans. It's an American favorite, and always thought of as quite a special treat toe eat.

Lasagna? In Italy the most popular Lasagna of all is Lasagna Bolognese made of course with a lush Bolognese Sauce and Bechamel with sprinklings of fresh grated Parmigiano Reggiano Cheese. The dish is absolutely heaven itself, and with the Bolognese recipe in this book you can make it. But as tasty as Lasagna Bolognese is, and we do love it, we Italian-Americans, especially in New York and out in Jersey love Lasagna this way. The recipe below has Lasagna made with layers of lasagna pasta, with home-made tomato sauce, fresh Ricotta Cheese, Parmesan, and Mozzarella. That's how we like it. There's another really awesome Lasagna that they make in Napoli called Lasagna Carnevale that is stuffed with Sausage and little Meatballs, and it's absolutely fabulous, but we're going to stick to this one, that's simply called Lasagna, and if you're Italian-American and live in New York or New Jersey, you know what it is.

If you've never made Lasagna before, then what are you waiting for? Every good cook must have this one in their repertoire, so here you go. Make it and enjoy it, and always remember to Mangia Bene. You've got Lasagna, you'll eat well for sure. Basta!

LASAGNA

INGREDIENTS For The SAUCE:

3 - 28 ounce cans Tomato Passata or crushed tomatoes or other good quality Italian style tomatoes
7 cloves minced garlic
1 small onion, minced
½ teaspoon crushed red pepper
¼ cup virgin olive oil
¼ chopped fresh basil or 1 teaspoon dried
Salt and pepper to taste

Remaining Ingredients:

2 lbs. Ronzoni (or other) boxes of Lasagna
2 ½ pound Whole Milk Ricotta
1 ½ pounds Mozzarella
2 ½ cups grated Parmigiano Reggiano
or Grana Padano

In a 6 quart or larger pot, sauté onions over a low flame for 3 minutes. Add garlic and cook for 3-4 minutes. Do not let the garlic get dark or burn.

Add tomatoes, turn heat up to high and stir. When sauce starts to bubble, turn flame down so the sauce is at a low simmer. Simmer for 45 minutes while frequently stirring the bottom of the pan to keep sauce from burning. Add fresh basil in the last ten minutes of cooking.

As the sauce is cooking, cook the lasagna sheets. Cook according to directions on lasagna package, but cook 1 minute less the instruction call for. Cook the lasagna in a large pot of rapidly boiling salted water.

Have a large bowl or pot of iced water on the side. As soon as the lasagna sheets are cooked according to instructions, remove from boiling water and place in ice water.

ASSEMBLING THE LASAGNA

Remove lasagna sheets from iced-water and let water drain off in a colander.

Dry the lasagna with a towel. This is very important, you don't want a soggy watery lasagna do you?

Shred or chop the Mozzarella in small pieces.

In a large bowl, mix eggs with the ricotta and ¼ of the grated Parmigiano.

In a 10 X 14 inch pan (or similar), coat the bottom of the pan with tomato sauce. Next, place sheets of lasagna lengthwise over tomato sauce. Cover the lasagna sheets with more sauce, and sprinkle on a little Parmigiano.

You will now place lasagna sheets that will go from the bottom and up the sides of the lasagna pan and over the sides. Place sheets on one side of the bottom of the pan and going up and draping over the sides of the pan. Later these sheets will be folded over the top. Do the same on the opposite side of the pan.

Place half of the ricotta cheese mixture as the next layer. Lay sheets of lasagna over the cheese lengthwise in the pan. Press down slightly on pasta. Spread a little tomato sauce over this layer of lasagna sheets, then sprinkle with Parmigiano. Repeat this step again with remaining ricotta to get the second and final layer of ricotta-mozzarella mixture.

Fold over the side lasagna sheets over the top layer on each side. Place the final layer of lasagna sheets over the top of the lasagna lengthwise. Spread tomato sauce over final sheets of pasta. Sprinkle on a generous amount of Parmigano.

Cover Lasagna loosely with aluminum foil and bake at 350 degrees for 40 minutes. Remove aluminum foil and bake a further 20 minutes at 375 degrees.

Remove Lasagna from oven and let rest for 30 minutes before serving. Once lasagna has cooled a bit, if you see that some water has seeped out on the sides, pick up the pan and pour off excess water into the sink.

IMPORTANT NOTES: Make sure that when you are assembling the Lasagna that you have two cups of Tomato Sauce leftover that you will heat up separately from the Lasagna and put some tomato sauce on the bottom of the plate you serve the lasagna on as well as draping a little Tomato Sauce over the top of the plated Lasagna and pass around grated cheese.

It is best to make your lasagna the night before serving. Cook the Lasagna, remove from oven. Let the Lasagna cool down at room temperature for about 90 minutes, then put in refrigerator a cool a few hours or overnight. To reheat the whole pan of lasagna, place in a 400 degree oven for 15 minutes, lower oven to 350 degrees and bake another 25 minutes. Remove from oven and let sit for 15 minutes before cutting and serving with heated Tomato Sauce and grated Parmigiano Reggiano. Enjoy!

NOTE II : Although for most pasta dishes nowadays we use a top quality imported Italian Pasta. When we we're growing up, my mother always and only used Ronzoni Brand Pasta. Now we use Italian pasta, all except in three instances; with Pastina, Jumbo Shells for Stuffed Shells, and when making Lasagna, we like to use Ronzoni *Sono Buoni.*

LASAGNA BOLOGNESE

Lasagna Bolognese? Well I wasn't going to put a recipe for this dish in the book, but then again, this book happens to be condensed cookbook of Italian-American favorites, but it's about Bolognese first. As I've already said, all the other recipes are an added bonus, and this recipe is one more. This Lasagna is the undisputed # 1 most famous Lasagna of any number of versions in Italy. In the World of Italian-America the Lasagna recipe preceding this is the most popular. And as for me, I do love Lasagna Bolognese every now and then, I much prefer to have my Bolognese with Spaghetti or Maccheroni. Anyway that's me. Everyone has there own taste and you may prefer this. So here it is, lasagna Bolognese. Buon Appetito!

RECIPE :

8 cups Ragu Bolognese from recipe in book (heated)
2 lbs. fresh Lasagna Pasta or dry if you can't get fresh
2 cups grated Parmigiano Reggiano

For BECHAMEL :

4 tablespoons Butter
4 tablespoons Flour
4 cups whole Milk

Heat the Milk in one small pan and set aside. Put the butter in another small pan and turn the heat on low. Once the butter has completely melted, add flour and whisk, while cooking on a low flame for 1-2 minutes. Do not brown.

Slowly whisk the milk into the flour a little at a time while whisking and cooking over low heat. Once all the milk is incorporated into the flour, add the salt and nutmeg. Continue cooking on low heat for 8-10 minutes, stirring with whisk every now and then. Turn heat off and set aside.

ASSEMBLING THE LASAGNA :

Cook all the Lasagna Pasta in rapidly boiling water until the pasta is slightly soft, yet slightly firm. If you have fresh pasta this will be about four minutes cooking. If you have dry lasagna pasta, it will be about 9-10 minutes.

As you are cooking the pasta have a large bowl with iced water to put the pasta into once you have finished cooking it. You not be cooking all the pasta all at once but in several batches. You will cook a few sheets, then remove from boiling water and put into the cold water to stop cooking. Do this until all the pasta is cooked.

Once the pasta has cooled, drain in a colander and shake off as much water as possible. Remove from colander. Pat the pasta dry with clean towels and set aside.

Rub the bottom of a 13 X 9 inch baking pan with half the butter. Spread a thin layer of the heated Bolognese Sauce over the bottom of the pan. The spread a thin layer of the Bechamel Sauce over the Bolognese Sauce. Sprinkle some of the grated Parmigiano over the Bechamel. Place a layer of Lasagna Pasta on top to completely cover. Repeat this process until you have 6 or 7 layers of Lasagna Pasta with the sauces in-between.

After the final layer of pasta, the top of the Lasagna should be Bolognese Sauce topped with Bechamel and grated Parmigiano on top that is dotted with the remaining half of the butter.

Bake in a 375 degree oven for 55 – 60 minutes. Remove from oven and let rest at least 20 minutes before serving.

MEATBALLS

Meatballs, who doesn't love them? Not many, I tell you, they are one of the greatest things ever! Yeah! Meatballs are *everyone's favorite dish*. Well, if not everyone, then certainly millions, that's for sure. Spaghetti & Meatballs, you know you love them too! And how about our beloved Meatball Parm? We have them every Monday, with some Meatballs we saved from the *Gravy* the day before. Meatballs, along with; Tomato Sauce, Sunday Sauce (Gravy), and Bolognese Sauce which are those dishes that if you're Italian-American, then you've just have to know how to make. Meatballs, they'll serve you and your family quite well. If you make them for dinner, no one will complain. Oh contraire, they'll all be happy as can be. Meatballs, make them for your Spaghetti & Meatballs dinner. Make a double batch, and you'll have plenty to make those prized Meatball Parm Sandwiches for lunch the next day. And maybe even the next day after that. Meatballs, you're gonna love them.

INGREDIENTS :

1 lb. ground Beef
½ lb. ground Veal
½ Pound Ground Pork
4 tablespoons fresh Italian Parsley, chopped
1 minced onion
2 cloves garlic, minced
4 tablespoons plain breadcrumbs
2 large eggs, ¼ cup Milk
Salt & pepper
½ cup grated Parmigiano or Grana Padano Cheese

Note: If you want, instead of this beef, pork, and veal proportions, you can use just Beef alone (2 pounds), or 1 lb. Ground Beef & 1 lb. Veal.

PREPARATION:

In a small bowl, break and beat eggs. Add breadcrumbs and milk and let soak for 10 minutes.

In a large bowl, add all the remaining ingredients. Add eggs and mix well with your hands.

Shape meat mixture to form balls that are about 2 inches in diameter.

Coat the bottom of a cookie sheet or roasting pan with a thin film of olive oil. Cook Meatballs at 350 degrees for 10 minutes.

Take the meatballs out of oven and simmer for 35 minutes in a batch of Tomato Sauce from the tomato sauce recipe in this book.

Serve Meatballs with Spaghetti for the Classic Italian-American favorite *Spaghetti & Meatballs* or do as the Italians do, especially the Neapolitans and serve the sauce first with Spaghetti, Rigatoni, or Ziti pasta. Then serve the Meatballs as the main course with a Salad or potatoes on the side.

And don't forget those tasty Meatball Parms the next day!

RIGATONI w/ SAUSAGE

We Italian-American's love our sausage. As a matter of fact we can't live without it. Some of us anyway. Our favorites are; our beloved Sausage & Pepper Sandwiches, Sausage & Peppers with Roast Potatoes, Orcechiette with Broccoli Rabe & Sausage, and this one, Rigatoni with Sausage. It's real easy to make, and you'll be set with an Italian favorite in just about 45 minutes time. Make a nice salad to precede the Pasta, and get yourself a good loaf of Italian Bread and you'll have a fine dinner that anyone is sure to love.

RECIPE :

1 - 28 ounce can of crushed Tomatoes
7 cloves minced garlic
1 small onion, minced
½ teaspoon crushed red pepper
8 tablespoons Olive Oil
¼ cup chopped fresh Basil
Salt and pepper to taste
10 Sweet Italian Sausage links
1 pound imported Italian Rigatoni
¼ cup grated Grana Padano or Pecorino Romano Cheese

Place sausages in a 6-quart pot and cover with water. Bring water to the boil and once it starts boiling, immediately lower the heat to low and let the sausages simmer on a low flame for 1o minutes.

Turn off heat and drain all water out of the pot. Leave the sausages in the pot, and add a little olive oil to coat the bottom of the pan. Cook sausages on medium heat until the sausages are lightly browned on all sides, about 6 minutes. Remove sausages from pot, and set aside.

Add garlic and a few tablespoons of olive oil to pot. Cook garlic on low heat until it just starts to get brown. About 4 minutes.

Add tomatoes to pot and turn heat to high. Once the tomatoes start to bubble, turn heat down to low and cook for 12 minutes.

While the tomato sauce is simmering, cut each link of sausage into 4 pieces each. Put the sausages into the sauce and let all simmer together for 12 minutes. Add the Basil into the pot for the last four minutes of cooking time. Turn heat off.

Cook the rigatoni according to the directions on package (about 12 minutes in rapidly boiling salted water). Once rigatoni is finished cooking, drain the pasta in a colander, reserving about 10 tablespoons of pasta cooking water.

Put the rigatoni back in the pot it cooked in with the reserved water. Add half the sausage sauce to pasta and mix. Plate the rigatoni onto 4 plates. Top each plate of pasta with an equal portion of remaining sauce and sausages.

Give each guest a plate of the Rigatoni w/ Sausages and pass around the grated cheese.

MAFALDINE with RABBIT RAGU

Rabbit, not everyone eats it I know. However there are a certain percentage who do, especially among older Italian guys who like it quite a bit. This ragu is a great way of enjoying rabbit with pasta, a dish that is especially popular in Tuscany and the island of Ischia in the Bay of Naples. If you've never had rabbit, you might want to give this one a try.

INGREDIENTS :

1 whole Rabbit, cut in 6 pieces
10 tablespoons Olive Oil
1 small Onion, peeled and minced
1 Carrot, peeled and chopped fine
2 Celery Stalks, chopped fine
3 ounces of Pancetta, chopped fine
¾ cup dry Red Wine, ¾ cup water
1 – 15 ounce can crushed Tomatoes
Salt & Black Pepper, 1 Bay Leaf
¼ cup fresh chopped Parsley
2 ounces dry Porcini Mushrooms, washed and soaked

Place the olive oil in a 6-quart pot and turn the heat on to high. Add the Rabbit and season the Rabbit with a little sprinkling of Salt & Pepper. Cook the Rabbit on medium-high heat until all the pieces are nicely browned on all sides, 10-12 minutes. Once the rabbit is nicely browned, remove from pan and set aside.

Add the Pancetta, onions, celery, and carrots to the pot and cook on low heat for 8 minutes while stirring. Add the wine to the pan and cook on high heat until the wine is reduced by half its original volume, about 6 minutes.

Add the tomatoes to pot and cook on high heat for 4 minutes. Add the water, the Porcini Mushrooms, Bay Leaf, ¼ teaspoon each of Salt & Black Pepper to the pot and turn heat on to high.

Add the rabbit pieces to the pot. Bring the liquid up to the boil, then lower the heat so the liquids are cooking at a low to medium simmer. Simmer the rabbit over low heat until the rabbit gets tender and is starting to pull away from the bone, about 1 hour and 25 minutes.

Remove the rabbit from the pot and let cool about 10 minutes. Once the rabbit has cooled, pull off all the meat from the bones and break in smaller pieces. Put this rabbit meat back into the pot. Cook over low heat for 15 minutes.

Cook your pasta according to the direction on the package. Once the pasta is cooked, quickly drain in a colander reserving ¼ cup of the pasta water to add to the sauce.

Place the pasta back in the pot it cooked in and drizzle on a few tablespoons of Olive Oil. Add heal the Rabbit Ragu to the pot with the pasta and mix. Plate the pasta onto 4-6 plates. Top each plate of pasta with a bit more of the sauce, sprinkle with chopped Parsley and serve. Pass around grated Parmesan or Grana Padano.

NOTE : To prepare the Dry Porcini Mushrooms, wash them, then place them in hot water to soak and reconstitute. Drain the mushrooms and chop.

FETTUCCINE ALFREDO

Once Upon a Time, this dish, Fettuccine Alfredo was hugely popular. People just loved it. The last several years or so, many Americans have become a lot more health conscience and turn their nose up at a dish like this made with quite a lot of cream. Yet, there are still people around who love this once very popular dish. It's funny, though this dish is super easy to make, not many people make it at home though they may love, they just eat in in restaurants. If however you love it as many still do, and you'd like to make it yourself, well here you go, the recipe is below.

INGREDIENTS :

1 lb. fresh Fettuccine
1 pt. heavy cream, ½ stick butter
1 cup grated Parmigiano Reggiano
2 egg yolks, salt & pepper

Put the cream in a large frying pan. Bring to the boil, lower the flame and let the cream cook. Season the cream with salt and pepper to taste. Reduce volume by One-Third, this will thicken the sauce.

Cook the fettuccine and drain it. Put the fettuccine in to the pan with the cream. Add butter and stir.

Turn the flame off. Add egg yolks and Parnigiano and stir. Serve and pass around extra Parmigiano.

PASTA CACIO e PEPE

Pasta Cacio Pepe is a wonderful Roman dish that's super easy to make, quick and easy and of course tasty as can be. In Rome it's usually made with Pecorino Cheese, put some prefer Parmigiano Reggiano or a combination of half Pecorino and half Parmigiano. Any way you make it, it is always good.

INGREDIENTS :

1 pound imported Italian Spaghetti or De Cecco Fettuccine
¾ stick of Butter, 6 tablespoons Olive Oil
1 cup Pecorino Romano Cheese
1 tablespoon coarsely ground Black Pepper

Cook the pasta in a pot of boiling salted water according to the direction on the package.

Place the Olive Oil and Butter in a large frying pan and cook on low heat until the butter is melted.

When the pasta is finished cooking, remove ½ cup of the pasta cooking water from the pan. Drain the pasta in a colander.

Add 1 cup of Pecorino Cheese, Black Pepper, and the half-cup of hot pasta water to the pan and mix, melting the cheese. Quickly add the pasta to the pan and mix with the cheese sauce.

Plate the pasta on four plates and serve to your guests. Pass around some grated Pecorino Romano for each diner to sprinkle over their Pasta Cacio Pepe. Enjoy.

SPAGHETTI w/ ARTICHOKES TOMATO & PEAS

INGREDIENTS :

2 pounds Baby Artichokes
¼ cup Olive Oil
6 Garlic cloves, peeled and sliced
¼ teaspoon Red Pepper Flakes
¼ teaspoon Salt, 1/3 teaspoon Black Pepper
15 Cherry Tomatoes, washed and cut in half
10 box of Frozen Peas, thawed
1 pound imported Italian Spaghetti or Short Maccheroni
¼ cup grated Pecorino Romano Cheese

Pull away outer green leaves of the Artichokes until you only see pale ones. Cut off green top. Cut off green bottom. Make sure there are no dark green pieces left. Cut each Baby Artichoke in-half from top to bottom.

Once all the artichokes are cut in half, boil in boiling salted water until the artichokes are tender yet slightly firm, about 4-5 minutes.

Place the Olive Oil and the artichokes in a medium size pot and cook at high heat until the artichokes start to get slightly browned, about 7 minutes. Season the artichokes with the Salt & Black Pepper and mix.

Add the garlic and Red Pepper and cook on medium heat for 2 minutes. Remove the artichokes from pan and set aside in a bowl or pan.
Add the Cherry tomatoes to the pot, season with a little salt and cook on high heat for 5 minutes. Add the Peas and cook for 2 minutes.

Cook the Pasta according to directions on the package.

Add the Artichokes back to the pot with the tomatoes and cook on low heat for 5 minutes.

Once the pasta is finished cooking, drain in a colander. Add the spaghetti to pot with the artichokes and mix. Plate the past on to 4-6 plates, giving each person and equal about of the Pasta, Artichokes, and Tomatoes. Pass the grated cheese and enjoy.

MACCHERONI
w/ *VEAL & MUSHROOM RAGU*

INGREDIENTS :

1 ½ pound of Veal Shoulder, cut into 1 ½" cubes
8 tablespoons olive oil
2 tablespoons Butter
2 ounces of Dry Porcini Mushrooms
1 small Onion, peeled and chopped fine
1 Carrot, peeled and chopped fine
8 ounces Button Mushrooms, washed and sliced
1 cup Dry White Wine
1 cup Chicken Broth
2 tablespoon Tomato Paste
1-pound short maccheroni such as Rigatoni or Cavatappi
Salt & Black Pepper
1 Bay Leaf
10 ounce box frozen Peas

Place the Olive Oil in a pot and turn heat on to high. Season the Veal with Salt & Black Pepper. Add Veal to pot and brown until the veal is golden brown all over, about 10 minutes.

Once the Veal is nicely browned, add the Celery, Onions, and Carrots to the pot and cook on medium heat for 5 minutes.

Remove the veal and the vegetables from the pot and place in a bowl. Add the Mushrooms & Butter to the pot and cook until the mushrooms get nicely browned. Remove the mushrooms and put in the bowl with the veal.

You should have nice brown bits sticking to the bottom of the pot. There's a lot of flavor in those brown bits that will give the sauce some nice flavor. Add the wine to the pot and cook on medium heat until the wine is reduced to half its original volume, about 5 minutes. As the wine reduces, you will be scraping the bottom of the pot with a wooden spoon to dislodge the brown bits on the bottom that will give the sauce lots of flavor.

Add the Veal, Mushrooms, and all the vegetables back to the pot. Add the Chicken Stock, Bay Leaf, Dry Porcini Mushrooms, and Tomato Paste to the pot with ¼ teaspoon each of Salt & Black Pepper and mix.

Bring the contents to the boil, then lower heat so everything is at a low to medium simmer. Simmer until the veal is nice and tender, 1 hour and 30 to 45 minutes.

Cook the maccheroni according to the directions on the package. As the maccheroni is cooking, add the peas to the Veal Ragu and let cook on low heat for two minutes.

Once the Maccheroni is finished cooking, drain it, reserving ¼ cup of water to add to the ragu and pasta.

Put the maccheroni back into the pot it cooked in with the reserved cooking water. Add half the Veal Ragu to the pot and mix with the pasta. Plate the pasta onto 4-6 plates and top each portion of pasta with more of the Mushroom Veal Ragu. Serve and enjoy.

BUCATINI alla MICHELANGELO

INGREDIENTS :

8 ounces Fresh Spinach, washed
½ cup Golden Raisons, soaked in hot water 15 minutes
6 tablespoons Olive Oil
1 tablespoon Butter
3 ounces Pignoli Nuts
1 ½ cups Ricotta Cheese
1/3 cup grated Parmigiano Reggiano or Grana Padano
1 pound Italian Bucatini (or Spaghetti or other Pasta)
¼ teaspoon Salt
¼ Black Pepper
Pinch of Nutmeg

Place the Olive Oil and Pignoli Nuts in a large skillet. Cook on medium heat until the Nuts begin to brown. Add butter and spinach and cook until Spinach begins to wilt, about 3 minutes.

Drop the Pasta into a large pot of boiling salted water and cook according to directions on package.

Take ¼ cup of water from pasta pot and add to pan with the spinach and cook on low heat 1 minute. Add the Salt, Pepper, Ricotta, and Nutmeg and cook on medium heat for 1 minute, then turn the heat off. Add most of the Grated Cheese to the pan with spinach and stir.

Once the pasta is finished cooking, drain into a colander. Put the pasta back in the pan it cooked in and add 2/3 of the spinach ricotta mixture to the past and mix.

Plate the pasta onto 4 plates and top with equal portions of the remaining spinach over the top of the pasta. Serve and pass some grated cheese. Buon Apettito.

RIGATONI con SUGO di OSSOBUCO
Pasta w/ Ossobuco Sauce

INGREDIENTS :

4 Veal Shanks
¼ cup Olive Oil
1 small Onion, peeled and diced
4 Carrots, peeled and chopped fine
2 Celery stalks, washed and minced fine
3 ounces Dry Porcini Mushrooms, washed
½ cups Dry Red Wine
1 – 28 can crushed Tomatoes
½ teaspoon Salt, ½ teaspoon ground Black Pepper
¾ cup Water or more if needed

Place the Dry Mushrooms in a small bowl of hot water and let soak Season both sides of each Veal Shank liberally with Salt & Black Pepper.

Place the half the Olive Oil in a medium pot and turn heat on to high. Place the Veal Shanks in the pot and cook on high heat until the Veal Shanks are nice and golden brown on each side, about 6-7 minutes each side. Once the Veal is browned on both sides remove from pot and set aside in a bowl.

Add the wine to the pot and cook on high heat as you scrape the bottom of the pan with a wooden spoon to dislodge the brown bits sticking to the bottom of the pan. Cook until the wine is reduced by half its original volumes. Pour the wine in the bowl with the Veal Shanks.

Add the remaining olive oil to the pot with the Onions, Celery, and Carrots and cook on medium heat for 6 minutes. Add the Garlic and cook on low heat for 2 minutes.

Turn heat on to high and let cook 30 seconds. Add the tomatoes and cook on high heat for 5 minutes while stirring.

Add the wine, water, and veal shanks back to the pot. Turn heat on to high and bring to the boil. Once the liquid comes to the boil, lower the heat to medium.

Drain the dry mushrooms and chop. Add the Mushrooms and Bay Leaf to pot. Cook the Veal Shanks on a low-medium simmer until tender and meat can easily pull away from the bone, about 1 hour and 45 minutes. Remove the veal from the pot and put in a bowl to cool for 15 minutes.

Pull the meat off the bone and break into smaller 1 ½" to 2" pieces and put back in the pot. Let cook on low heat for 15 minutes on low heat.

This amount of Ossobuco Ragu is enough for at least 12-14 portions of pasta, so if you're cooking a pound of pasta you'll just need a fraction of this sauce and put the rest in containers in the refrigerator to eat on another day or two.

MACCHERONI w/ PORK RAGU

INGREDIENTS :

2 pounds Pork Spare Ribs, cut into 2 rib pieces
¼ cup Olive Oil
6 cloves Garlic, peeled and sliced
1 small Onion, peeled and chopped fine
1 – 28 ounce can crushed Tomatoes
1 – 28 ounce can Tomato Passata (Tomato Puree)
Salt & Black Pepper
¼ teaspoon Red Pepper Flakes
¾ cup dry Red Wine, 2 Bay Leaves
1 pound Rigatoni, Cavatappi, or any short pasta you like
¼ cup grated Pecorino Romano or Grana Padano Cheese

Place 8 tablespoons of the Olive Oil in a 8-quart pot and turn heat on to high. Season the Ribs with a little Salt & Black Pepper and brown in two separate batches. Get a nice golden brown color on all the ribs, about 8 minutes per batch.

Remove the ribs from the pot and set aside in a large bowl or pan.

Add the wine to the pot and cook on high heat scraping the bottom of pot to dislodge the brown bits on the bottom of the pot. Cook the wine until it has reduce to half its original volume, about 4-5 minutes. Pour the wine into the pan with the ribs.

Add remaining Olive Oil and the Onions to the large pot and cook on medium heat for 5 minutes. Lower heat to low and add the Garlic and Red Pepper and cook for 2 minutes on low heat.

Turn the heat to high and add the crushed tomatoes and cook on high heat for 4 minutes while stirring. Add the Tomato Passata (Puree), the Ribs, the reduced wine, and Bay Leaves. Add ½ teaspoon each of Salt & Black Pepper. Turn the heat to high. Once the contents comes to the boil, lower the heat to a low-medium simmer and cook the ribs and sauce until the ribs are tender and start pulling away from the bone, about 1 hour and a half to 1 hour and 45 minutes. Make sure that you stir the sauce every now and then, scraping the bottom of the pot with a wooden spoon. Also, if the sauce starts getting to thick, just add a little water as needed to loosen the sauce a bit.

Once the Ribs are cooked and are tender, remove from the pot and set aside to cool for about 12 minutes. Pull all the meat off the rib Bones and put into the pot with the sauce (Ragu). Simmer on low heat for 15 minutes.

After the Rib Meat has been simmering for 5 minutes, start cooking the pasta of your choice in boiling salted water according to the directions on the package.

When the pasta has cooked, drain in a colander and reserve ¼ cup of the pasta cooking water. Put the pasta back in the pot it cooked in and drizzle on some additional Olive Oil. Add some of the Pork Ragu to the pasta pot and mix.

Plate the pasta in equal portions on 4 separate plates. Top the pasta with some more of the Pork Ragu, serve and pass around the grated cheese.

MACCHERONI w/ SAUSAGE & PEAS

INGREDIENTS :

1 medium Onion, peeled and chopped
6 tablespoons Italian Olive Oil
1 lb. of Sweet Italian Sausage, removed from casing and crumbled
1 cup Tomato Passata (or Tomato Sauce you made from)
¾ cup Water
¼ teaspoon each of Kosher Salt & Black Pepper
¼ teaspoon dry Basil
2 – 10 ounce boxes of Frozen Peas
1 pound Conchiglie Maccheroni (Small Shells)
1/3 cup grated Parmigiano Reggiano

Place the onions and Olive Oil in a medium sized pot. Cook onions on medium heat for 4 minutes.

Add the Sausage and cook until the Sausage meat loses its raw color. Add the Tomatoes, Salt, Pepper, dry Basil, and water and cook on low heat for 25 minutes, stirring occasionally and making sure the sauce doesn't stick to the bottom of the pan. You can add a little more water if the sauce starts to get too thick. After the sauce has been cooking 20 minutes add Peas to pot and continue cooking.

After the sauce has been cooking about 12 minutes, add the pasta to a pot of boiling salted water and cook according to directions on the package. When done, drain the pasta in a colander, reserving a little of the pasta cooking water.

After the sauce has cooked for 25 minutes, turn the heat off. Add the Maccheroni to the pot with the sauce and mix. Drizzle on a little olive oil and ¼ cup of the pasta cooking water and mix. Add half the cheese and mix. Plate the Maccheroni onto 4-6 plates and serve. Pass the grated Parmigiano and enjoy, e Mangia Bene.

SAUSAGE MEATBALLS w/ RICE
Riso con Polpette di Salsiccia

This is a dish that some Italians in the New York Metro area like to eat. It's kind of rare, so you may not have heard of it, but those of us who eat it, just love it, and you're sure to like it too. The recipe is below, so if you're looking for something a little different and new, give this a whirl. The recipe is below, it's quite tasty for sure and real easy to make. We hope you'll enjoy.

INGREDIENTS :

1 ½ pounds Sweet Italian Sausage, casings removed
2 cups Long Grain Rice
4 cups water
2 Bouillon Chicken Cubes
½ cup grated Grana Padano or Parmigiano Cheese
¼ cup fresh chopped Italian Parsley
¼ teaspoon Kosher Salt
¼ teaspoon ground Black Pepper
1 tablespoon Butter, Bay Leaf
1 pinch Spanish Saffron

Place Bouillon Cubes, the water, and Bay Leaf in a medium pot. Turn heat on to high and bring to the boil.

Place the sausage meat in a bowl with; Black Pepper, half the Parsley, and half of the grated cheese. Mix all very well with your hands, the shape meat into golf-ball sized Meatballs.

Once all the Sausage Meatballs have been formed, place them in the chicken broth and let cook at a low simmer until the meatballs are fully cooked, about 8-10 minutes.

Remove meatballs from oven and put in a pan in a 200 degree oven to keep them warm.

Add saffron, butter, and rice to the broth that the meatballs cooked in. Cook the rice at a very low simmer for 16 minutes. Turn heat off, cover the rice with a top or with a piece of aluminum-foil and let sit for 5 minutes.

Add the remaining Cheese and Parsley to the rice and stir to mix all together. Put the rice into a coffee cup and pack in. Take coffee cup and put onto a shallow soup bowl or place and let the rice fall out, forming a mound of rice that has taken the shape of the cup.

Place 5 or 6 Meatballs around the rice and serve.

ZUPPA di LENTICCHE alla DANIELE
My Famous Sausage & Lentil Soup

Has anyone ever asked you what's your favorite thing to eat, or what's your favorite anything? Of course they have, we're asked this question all the time. It's part of life. Sometimes you know right a way, depending on the subject; what's your favorite color, who was your favorite teacher, girlfriend, sports-figure, football team, whatever. So what's your favorite soup. Now some things I can tell you right away and others I have to ponder, as with soup, as there are a few that I love quite a bit. Those favorite soups of mine would be; Manhattan Clam Chowder, Pasta Fagioli, Italian Wedding Soup, and yes Zuppa di Lenticchie or as most Americans know it as Lentil Soup. It's a tough choice, but when I really think about it, it comes down to Lentil Soup, but not just any Lentil Soup but mine, Zuppa di Lenticchie alla Daniele, yes Daniel's Lentil Soup. Why is it so good? Well for one it taste good. Two it's inexpensive and easy to make. That's three. And four, it's got wonderful Sweet Italian Sausages in it. Now what's better than that? Well I tell you something else. When you make a pot of this lentil soup or any soup for that matter, it's easy to make, you make a big pot of it, and you've got food for a few days. You make it, then eat a bowl, and put the rest away, into the refrigerator and the next few days when you need something to eat?

There it is, the Lentil Soup is in the frig. Pull it out, put some in a pot, heat it up and in a few minutes you're eating dam well. It's Lentil Soup, and you made it. Buon Appetito!

LENTIL SOUP The RECIPE :

1 pound dry Lentils, washed
1 large Onion, peeled and chopped
¼ cup Olive Oil
2 stalks Celery, washed and chopped
3 Carrots, peeled and cut to 1 " cubes
1 large Potato, peeled and cut to 1" cubes
6 cloves Garlic, peeled and minced
4 quarts water, 2 Chicken Bullion Cubes
6 San Marzano Tomatoes, chopped
1 Bay Leaf
4 ounces imported Italian Ditalini Pasta (or Ronzoni)
8 Italian Sweet Sausages

Put olive oil, Onions, and Celery in a large 8 quart non-corrosive pot and sauté at low heat for 6 minutes.

Add the Garlic and cook for two minutes more.

Add tomatoes and cook on high heat for 3 minutes.

Add lentils, water, and Bullion Cube if using. Bring up to the boil. Once the liquid is up to the boil, lower heat to medium simmer and cook for 18 minutes.

Meanwhile, cook the sausages in a pan of low simmering water for 10 minutes. Remove and add to pot with the lentils.

Let the lentils continue cooking for another 10 minutes, until they are tender, yet slightly firm and the sausages are cooked through. Turn heat off.
Remove the sausages from the pot and let cool on a plate for a few minutes. Cut sausage into ½" thick pieces and add to the soup.

Ladle the soup into soup bowls, drizzle a little olive oil on top and pass some grated cheese to your guest and yourself.

NOTE: Omit the Sausages and Bullion Cubes from this recipe to make a regular Lentil Soup that is meatless and suitable for vegetarians and during the Lenten Season. You can eat it as is, or add some Escarole for the always-popular Lentil & Escarole Soup. It's oh so good.

BONUS !!! Here's another two-in-one recipe for you. So you've made this soup and already ate some. Of course you have, it's delish. Guess what? You can have something a little different and a Big Time Italian-American New Yorkers favorite. What you ask? It's Pasta Lenticchie, my cousin Joe's favorite and something my Nonna Giuseppina made my mother and uncles all the time.

To make Pasta Lenticchie, you cook some pasta. We like ours with Gemelli. Heat up some of the Zuppa di Lenticchie that you've drained some water out of, as this will now be a sauce as opposed to a soup. Once you have cooked your pasta, strain it in a colander, reserving a little of the pasta cooking water. Put the pasta back in the pot it cooked in. Put in half the Lentils that you've heated into the pot with the pasta. Drizzle on a little olive oil and mix the Pasta & Lentils together. Give everyone a nice plate that is topped with more of the Lentils. Pass around grated Pecorino Romano and enjoy, you got Pasta Lenticchie, a New York Italian favorite. What's better than that?

ZUPPA di POLLO alla SICILIANA
Sicilian Chicken & Vegetable Soup

Many Americans might not realize how big soups are in the realm of Italian cooking. Most non Italian Americans think of Pasta and Pizza first with Veal dishes, Sausages and Meatballs as well, but not usually of soup. For my family and most other Italian immigrant families of the late 1800's and first half of the 20th Century soups were huge. Along with pasta, soups were the cheapest and easiest dishes of all. My Sicilian Grandmother served her family soup almost everyday. She often served Zuppa di Lenticchie (Lentil Soup) most of all, as it was cheaper than anything else. If she had a bit more money she would make this hearty satisfying soup three or four times a months and would get at least two full meals out of it to serve her family of seven which included her husband, herself, daughters Lilly and Lucia (my mother), and sons; James, Tony, and Frank. This soup is a winner, I'm sure you'll agree.

RECIPE :

1 whole broiler Chicken (about 3 pounds) washed
2 medium onions, peeled and diced
5 Carrots, peeled and cut in ¾" cubes
3 stalks Celery, washed and diced
7 cloves Garlic, peeled and sliced

2 large Baking Potatoes, peeled and cut to ¾" cubes
1 – 12 ounce package of Frozen Peas
1 – 14 ounce can of Crushed Tomatoes
1 – 14 can Cannellini Beans, drained and washed
5 ounces Ditalini or other short pasta
½ to 3/4 teaspoon Salt (Sicilian Sea Salt if possible)
½ teaspoon ground Black Pepper
1 Bay Leaf
Water

Place Olive Oil and onions in a large pot. Cook on low heat for seven minutes. Add garlic, and cook 3 minutes on low heat.

Add tomatoes and cook on high heat until tomatoes start bubbling. Turn heat to low and let cook for 6 minutes on low heat. Remove from pan and set aside till later.

Add chicken and Bay Leaf to pot that you cooked the tomatoes and onion in. Fill the pot with water to cover the chicken by 1 inch. Turn heat up to high. Once the water starts boiling, turn heat to low and let simmer for 15 minutes.

Add the tomatoes to pot, along with the potatoes, celery, and carrots. Bring back to the boil. Once the liquid starts boiling again, turn flame down so the liquid is at a low to medium simmer. Let simmer for 1 hour more.

Remove the chicken from pot and let it cool down for about 12 minutes.

Cook the Ditalini (or other pasta) according to directions on package. Drain pasta in colander, then run under cold water for 2 minutes. Shake water off pasta and set aside.

Once the chicken has cooled, remove all the meat from the chicken, break into small pieced and put back in the pot with the broth. Discard chicken skin and bones.

Add the cooked pasta and cannellini beans to soup and let cook on a low flame for 6 minutes. Add frozen peas and let cook for 3 minutes. The soup is now ready to serve.

Buon Appetito!

MINESTRONE alla GENOVESE

INGREDIENTS :

¼ cup Olive Oil
2 medium Onions, peeled and chopped
6 cloves Garlic, peeled and chopped
¼ teaspoon crushed Red Pepper Flakes
4 Celery stalks, washed and chopped
6 medium Carrots, peeled and cut in 1 ½ inch dice
3 large Baking Potatoes, peeled and cut into ¼" slices
3 medium Zucchini, washed and cut into 1 ½ " dice
half pound Green Beans, cut off ends, then cut in half
1 – 12 ounce package of frozen Peas
5 ounces Ditalini Pasta
water
1 tablespoon Sea Salt
1 tablespoon ground Black Pepper
2 Bay Leafs
1 pint Cherry Tomatoes cut in half
1 tablespoon Pesto for every portion served (recipe in book)

Put first 5 ingredients in a large 8-quart pot and sauté over low heat for 8 minutes. Add Cherry Tomatoes and cook on high heat for 7 minutes.

Add potatoes, bay leaf, and carrots and cover all with water to 3 inches above the vegetables. Cook on high heat for 20 minutes.

Cook pasta in boiling water while soup is cooking. Drain when finished and set aside.

Add the zucchini and green beans and continue cooking the soup on high heat for 12 minutes. Add peas and cook 5 minutes.

The soup is ready. Fill soup bowls with the soup and top each bowl of soup with 1 tablespoon of Basil Pesto. Enjoy!

GARLIC OREGANO CHICKEN

This is a tasty and oh so easy to make chicken dish that every just loves. It's more or less a one-pot meal, which everyone loves as well. You got your chicken and potatoes that roast together with the chicken, and it's quite awesome just like this. If you like you serve a salad beforehand or a little on the plate with the chicken and everyone is just sure to love it. Enjoy.

INGREDIENTS :

1 – 3 lb. Broiler Chicken cut into 8 pieces and washed
8 tablespoons Olive Oil
12 cloves Garlic, peeled and left whole
½ teaspoon Kosher or Sea Salt
½ teaspoon ground Black Pepper
1 ½ tablespoons dry Oregano
2 large Baking Potatoes, washed
¼ cup water
¼ cup chopped fresh Italian Parsley (optional)

Cut each potato in-half lengthwise, the cut each half across the width into 6 pieces each.

Place all the ingredients except the water and Parsley in a glass or ceramic baking pan. Mix thoroughly together to coat all the chicken and potatoes with the olive oil, salt, pepper, and Oregano.

Place in a 400 degree oven with the skin-side up on the chicken. Cook at 400 degree for 12 minutes. Remove from oven and turn chicken pieces over. Lower the heat to 350 degrees and cook for 20 minute.

Remove chicken from the oven and turn the chicken over again, so the skin side is up. Turn the heat back to 400 degrees and cook chicken for 10 minutes at 400 degrees.

Remove the chicken from the oven and let it rest 10-12 minutes before serving.

This amount of chicken will serve 2 to four people, depending on how hungry everyone is and whatever else they might be eating with the meal.

To serve more people, you can simply double this recipe using 2 chickens and four potatoes, and if you like, you can also make some carrots or a nice green vegetable to go along with the Chicken and Potatoes.

JOHN'S CACCIATORE SEGRETO

This is the tastiest recipe for Chicken Cacciatore that I've ever seen or tasted anywhere. I worked as a Waiter and Bartender at the famous 100 year old Italian Red Sauce Restaurant, John's on East 12th Street for 7 years. John's is a great old-school Italian Joint that's been operating on East 12th Street Since 1908 and has seen the likes of Lucky Luciano, John Lennon, Ray Davies, and The Ramones walk through its doors. They make awesome Baked Clams Oreganata, the Best Speedino Mozzarella in town, and this, the best Chicken Cacciatore I've ever tasted anywhere anytime.

NOTE : Most recipes for Chicken Cacciatore are made with the chicken being braised in a good amount of tomatoes. As with most recipes there are numerous versions, thus this recipe that doesn't use tomato at all. You'll find this dish richer and deeper in flavor than it is with the tomato.

The SECRET RECIPE :

1 small broiler Chicken, about 3 pounds
1 Red Bell Pepper, washed
6 tablespoons Olive Oil
¼ cup Sweet Marsala Wine
¼ teaspoon each Salt & Black Pepper
6 ounce Button Mushrooms, washed and cut into quarters

Cut chicken into 8 pieces, 2 legs, to breasts, 2 thighs, and two wings. Season both sides of all the chicken with a little salt and Black Pepper. Set chicken aside.

Cut the Red Bell Pepper in-half and remove seeds and pith and discard. Cut each half into ¼" strips. Place the Olive Oil and Peppers in a large frying pan and cook the peppers on low heat for 8 minutes.

Add the Mushrooms to the pan with the Bell Peppers and sprinkle all with a little salt and pepper. Cook on medium-high heat until all the mushrooms are nicely browned, about 8 minutes. Remove the mushrooms and peppers from the pan and set aside.

Place a little Olive Oil in pan to coat it and turn the heat on high. Add chicken to pan skin-side down and cook on high heat until the chicken is nicely golden brown, about 7 minutes. Turn chicken over and cook on other side 6-7 minutes.

Turn chicken over again and add the Marsala Wine to pan. Cook on low heat for 7 minutes. Turn the chicken over so the skin side is up and cook on low heat for 8 minutes. If chicken starts getting a little dried-out, add a little water to the pan.

Turn heat off, add the butter to the pan and swirl around. Let the chicken rest for seven minutes before serving. Serves two to three people. To serve more, just double the amounts of this recipe.

POLLO ZINGARA

INGREDIENTS :

4 skinless boneless Chicken Breasts
10 tablespoons Olive Oil
8 ounce Button Mushrooms, washed and sliced
1 small Onion, peeled and sliced thin
1 small Yellow Bell Pepper, seeded and sliced thin
8 Asparagus
¾ cup Tomato Sauce (from recipe in book)
Salt & Black Pepper to taste
1 cup flour, ¼ cup dry White Wine
2 tablespoons Butter, ¼ cup fresh chopped Italian Parsley

Cut tough bottom piece off each Asparagus. The cut the each Asparagus on an angle into 5 pieces each. Place the asparagus in a small pot of salted boiling water and cook for 3 minutes. Drain the asparagus in a colander and run cold water over the asparagus for 2 minutes to cool. Leave in colander and set aside.

Place half the Olive Oil and the sliced peppers in a large frying pan and cook on medium heat for 7 minutes. Place the onions in the pan and cook with the peppers on medium heat for 4 minutes. Season with a pinch of Salt & Black Pepper.

Remove the peppers and onions from the pan and set aside. Add the Mushrooms and half the butter to the pan and cook the Mushrooms on medium-high heat until they get browned, about 7 minutes. Season with salt and pepper and mix. Remove the mushrooms from the pan and put aside with the yellow peppers.

Season both sides of each Chicken Breast with a pinch of Salt & Black Pepper each. Dredge both sides of each breast in the flour that has been place in a shallow bowl. Shake off excess flour.

Put remaining Olive Oil in the pan and turn the heat to medium high. Add the remaining butter to the pan. Cook the chicken in the pan until lightly browned and cooked through, about 3 minutes on each side

Remove chicken from pan and set aside. Add wine to pan and cook on high heat as you scrape the bottom of pan with a wooden spoon and the wine is reduced by half its original volume, about 4 minutes.

Add all the vegetables back to the pan with the tomato sauce and cook on medium heat 3 minutes. Add the chicken and half the Parsley to the pan and cook on low heat for 2 minutes.

To serve place Chicken Breasts onto 4 plates. Top each chicken breast with and even amount of the sauce and sprinkle remaining parsley over the four plates, and Mangia Bene.

PORK CUTLETS MILANESE

Veal Milanese is one of both Italy's and Italian-America's favorite dishes. One thing though about Veal Milanese, veal is quite expensive, thus is Veal Milanese. If you love Veal Milanese, but don't like the price, here's a solution for you. It's something we Italian-Americans like to do, make the dish with Pork or Chicken instead of the very expensive veal and you all set to go.

INGREDIENTS :

4 Center Cut Pork Cutlets
2 Eggs
½ cup All Purpose Flour
1 cup Plain Breadcrumbs
1 teaspoon Salt
1 teaspoon ground Black Pepper
4 tablespoons Milk
¼ cup Canola Oil
2 tablespoons butter

Get the separate bowls and lay out on a table. Fill one bowl with the flour, 1 with breadcrumbs, and one with the eggs.

Add one-third each of the Salt & Black Pepper to each one of these bowls and mix. Add milk to the eggs and beat.

Season each pork cutlet on each side with a little salt & pepper.

One by one, take each pork cutlet and dredge in bowl with flour. Shake off excess flour and place in the bowl with the beaten eggs.

Cover the cutlet completely with the beaten egg, remove from eggs, shake off excess egg, then place in the bowl with the breadcrumbs. Cover the cutlet completely with breadcrumbs, pressing the breadcrumbs into the cutlet. Repeat until all f cutlets are breaded.

Place oil and butter in a medium skillet and turn heat to high.

Fry each breaded Pork Cutlet, on-by-one in the hot oil & butter until they are a light colored golden brown on each side.

Remove from hot oil and place on clean paper towels to soak up a bit of the oil.

Place the cutlets on four plates with a large wedge of lemon on each plate and top the Fried Cutlets with a little Arugala & Cherry Tomato Salad.

ARUGALA SALAD

4 bunches of Baby Arugala
16 Cherry Tomatoes, washed and cut in half

Place arugala & tomatoes in a small bowl, add 5 tablespoons of Olive Oil and 4 teaspoons fresh lemon juice with ¼ teaspoon each of Salt & Black Pepper, mix and top the Pork Milanese with this salad, and Voila, you've got Maialle alla Milanese. Buon Appetito e Mangia Bene!

PORCHETTA

Porchetta is one of the tastiest most savory dishes anyone could ever dream of eating. A Porchetta is a boneless whole roast pig that has been seasoned with Garlic, Fennel, rosemary and other herbs until tenderly delicious. This wonder of Italian Gastronomy is found all over Italy these days, originating in Lazio and the eternal city of Rome. It is also prevalent throughout Central Italy especially in the regions of Tuscan and Umbria. As I've said it can be found all over Italy and I'll never forget the Porchetta Sandwiches that me and my buddy Jimmy Starace had one day in Verona after we came out of the huge wine exposition known as Vinitaly. We came out of the show and there was Porchetta stand right outside the venue. I told Jimmy, "hey we gotta get some Porchetta Sandwiches." We did, and of course they were absolutely awesome and me and Jimmy Boy were quite happy eating them after a day of drinking mass quantities of Italian Wine. This was one of those wonderful little incidents I'll never forget. Good times eating Italian Food and drinking the wine, "Mangia e Beve."

INGREDIENTS :

¼ cup Olive Oil
¼ cup Fennel Fronds
7 sprigs Rosemary, leaves removed from stems
8 Sage leaves, chopped
6 cloves Garlic, Peeled
1 teaspoon Fennel Seeds
zest of one Lemon
1 ½ teaspoons Kosher Salt
¾ teaspoons Black Pepper
½ teaspoon Red Pepper Flakes
1 whole-Pork Shoulder with skin on (about 6-7 pounds)
2 large Onions, peeled and sliced thickly

Put first 10 ingredients in a food processor and pulse until all are thoroughly mixed into a paste, about 2 minutes.

Place the onions in a large baking pan and drizzle a little Olive Oil over the onions. Rub the paste completely all over the pork shoulder. Cover with plastic wrap in put in the refrigerator to marinate for 3-4 hours or over night.

Remove the Pork Shoulder from the refrigerator at least 1 hour before putting in the oven. Heat oven to 400 degrees 15 minutes before you will be putting the pork in.

Roast the Pork for 30 minutes at 400 degrees. Lower the oven to 350 degrees and roast the pork until done, about 2 hours and 45 minutes to 3 hours, until a meat thermometer stuck into the Pork reads 175 degrees.

Remove from oven and let rest 15 minutes before serving. Cut the Porchetta into thick slices and serve with Roast Potatoes or whatever vegetable you like, or of course the Porchetta makes one of the World's Great Sandwiches, just slice some and put onto good Italian Bread or Hero Rolls, and you're gonna go out of your mind at the *other-worldly* taste of it all

STEAK & ONIONS

We Italians might eat a lot of pasta, some almost every day. This said, we do love a nice juicy Sirloin Steak every now and then. Two things with Steak, you've got to get Prime Meat, and you've got to now how to cook it right. First off, never use a home-stove broiler. The best and very good way to cook a steak at home is in a heavy-bottom pan that you can get nice and hot. Oh yes, # 2, you've got to know what you're doing. You have to season your steak liberally with salt and pepper, cook it on high heat to get it properly browned, and you're all set. Some like their Italian Steak alla Pizzaiola, if you do, that recipe follows this one. You might also like your steak with some nicely sautéed mushrooms over the top. So go ahead and try this recipe below, you're sure to love it.

INGREDIENTS :

2 medium Onions, peeled and sliced
2 Prime Sirloin Steaks cut 1 ½ inches each
6 tablespoons Olive Oil
Kosher or Salt and ground Black Pepper to taste
2 ½ tablespoons Butter
2 tablespoons fresh chopped Italian Parsley

Place half the butter and 4 tablespoons of the olive oil and a medium sized heavy bottom skillet. Add the onions and cook on low heat for about 15 minutes, until the onions get nice and golden brown, but not burned. After the onions have been cooking about 8 minutes season with ¼ teaspoon each of Slat & Pepper and continue cooking.

When onions are finished cooking remove from heat, put in a bowl and set aside.

Liberally season both sides of each steak with a good amount of salt & pepper. Add remaining olive oil to the pan and turn heat to high. Add steaks to pan and cook on high heat for 3 minutes. Turn heat down to medium and cook 2 minutes. Turn the steaks over and cook on high heat for two minutes. Turn heat to medium and cook two minutes more on medium heat.

Remove steaks from pan and let rest on a plate for 5 minutes before serving. Meanwhile put onions back in the pan and cook on very low heat for 5 minutes while the steak is resting. Turn heat off. Add remaining butter to pan with the onions and mix.

Plate the steaks onto two plates. Divide the onions in half and drape over the steaks. Sprinkle a little Parsley over the onions if you're using and enjoy those steaks. Serve with the Tuscan Garlic Potatoes below, sautéed greens or whatever you like.

STEAK PIZZAIOLA

INGREDIENTS :

2 Prime Sirloin Steaks, cut 1" thick
4 tablespoons Olive Oil
5 cloves Garlic, peeled and sliced
1 medium Onion, peeled and sliced
1 Red Bell Pepper, cleaned and sliced
Pepperoncino (Red Pepper Flakes)
2 cups crushed Tomato
½ cup water
Kosher Salt
Black Pepper
Oregano
¼ cup fresh chopped Parsley

Season the Steaks liberally with Salt & Black Pepper. Put olive oil in a heavy-bottom frying pan and turn heat on high. Cook The Steaks until nice and brown, about 2 ½ minutes on each side.

Remove steaks from pan and set aside. Add the Red Bell Peppers and cook on medium heat for 5 minutes. Add the onions and cook on low heat for 6 minutes with the peppers. Season the peppers and onions with salt & black pepper and mix.

Add Red Pepper Flakes, Garlic, and Oregano to pan and cook on low heat for 3 minutes. Add the tomatoes and water and a pinch more of salt & black pepper to pan. Turn heat to high and cook for 2 minutes on high heat. Lower heat to medium and cook for seven minutes.

Put the steaks back in the pan with tomatoes and cook on medium heat until steaks are Medium Rare, about 7-8 minutes.

Remove steaks from pan and let rest for five minutes. Continue cooking the tomatoes fro 5 minutes on low heat.

Slice the steaks across the grain. To serve, place half the sauce on each of two to three plates. Divide the steak among the plates and arrange nicely over the sauce. Put a little more sauce down the middle of each plate of steak. Drizzle a little Olive Oil and Parsley over the steaks and serve.

NOTE : Have whatever you like to go with the steak; Sautéed Broccoli Rabe, Salad, or the Tuscan Garlic Potatoes below.

CHICKEN FRANCESE

Chicken Francese, now isn't that *Fancy?* Chicken Francese used to be a popular dish back in the 1960's & 70's .. Chicken Francese is a hugely popular dish in Rochester New York, so much so that some have suggested the dish be called Chicken Rochester. As of this date, that has not happened. It is said that Italian Immigrants to Rochester brought their recipes with them, including Veal Francese and substituted chicken for the more expensive Veal in Veal Francese. The rest is history.

INGREDIENTS :

4 skinless boneless Chicken Breast
1 cup Flour
½ teaspoon each of Salt & Black Pepper
3 Eggs
¼ cup Canola Oil (or any Vegetable Oil)
½ stick Butter
1/3 cup Dry White Wine
¼ cup water
¼ cup fresh chopped Parsley
2 Lemons, juice one and cut the other into thin slices

Place the chicken breast between 2 pieces of plastic wrap and pound with a meat mallet until all the breast are ¼" thick.

Season both sides of each chicken breast with salt & pepper.

Place the flour in one shallow bowl with ½ teaspoon each of salt & pepper and mix.

Place the eggs in another shallow bowl, season with salt & pepper and beat the eggs. Place the oil in a large skillet and heat to high.

Dredge each piece of chicken in the flour, shake off excess four and then dip in to the eggs and coat completely. Shake off excess egg and put immediately into the pan with the hot oil. Do this with all four pieces of chicken.

Cook the chicken for two minutes on each side, then remove from pan and place on paper towels and keep warm.

Drain off all the oil from the pan.

Add the water, wine, and Lemon Juice to pan and cook on high heat until the liquid is reduced by half, about 5 minutes.

Turn the heat of and add the butter and chopped Parsley to the pan and swirl the pan in a circular direction to emulsify the sauce.

Place the Chicken Breast onto four plates. Pour the sauce over each chicken breast, and top the chicken with Lemon slices and serve.

SICILIAN CHICKEN

Here's a dish my mom used to make all the time. She leaned how to make it from her mother, my maternal grandmother Giuseppina Bellino who immigrated from Lercara Friddi, Sicily to New York with my grandfather Philipo in 1904 .. This is a nice tasty chicken dish that's hearty and easy to make. Serve it as is with the onions and potatoe, and if like you can throw in some mushrooms and or carrots as well, as the chicken is cooking.

INGREDIENTS :

1 – 3 pound Chicken, cut into 8 pieces
12 tablespoons Olive Oil
2 medium Onions, peeled and sliced
3 Baking Potatoes, peeled and cut to 1 ½" dice
¼ teaspoon each of Salt & Black Pepper
2 sprigs fresh Rosmary 8 tablespoons chopped fresh Parsley
1/3 cup dry White Wine
1 cup water

Cut the Chicken into 8 pieces yielding; 2 breasts, 2 thighs, 2 legs, and 2 wings. Season the chicken with a little Salt & Black Pepper on each piece.

Place the Olive Oil in a large skillet and turn the heat on high. Cook the chicken on medium-high heat until all the chicken is nicely golden brown on all sides, about 10-12 minutes. Remove the chicken from the pan and set aside on a platter or pan.

Turn the heat on high, add the potatoes, season with a pinch of salt & pepper and cook until the potatoes are nicely browned, about 8 minutes.

Remove the potatoes from the pan and set aside with the chicken.

Add the onions to the pan and cook over low heat until the potatoes are a nice deep brown color, being careful not to burn, about 12-14 minutes. Remove the onions and set aside.

Add the wine to the pan and cook on medium heat until the wine is reduced by half, about 4 minutes. Add the chicken back to pan with the rosemary laid on top.

Place half the onions on top of the chicken and season with a tiny pinch of Salt & Pepper. Place half the potatoes on top of the onions, then another layer of onions and top with the remaining potatoes to make a layer of the chicken on bottom and two alternating layers of Potato & Onions.

Place the water in the pan and turn heat to high. Once the water starts to bubble, cover the pan with a lid and low the flame to low and cook the chicken on low heat until it is cook through and falling off the bone, about 35-40 minutes.

As the chicken is cooking, check from time to time, if it is getting dry out, you can add a bit more water to the pan as needed. In the last 5 minutes of cooking add half the parsley to the pan.

When the chicken is finished cooking turn the heat off. Plate the Chicken on four plates, dividing the chicken, onions, and potatoes evenly among the 4 plates. Sprinkle remaining Parsley over the chicken and serve. Eat the chicken just like this or serve with a nice green vegetable as well. Enjoy.

VEAL & PEPPER

Remember in the great Martin Scorsese movie Goodfellas when Ray Liotta (Henry Hill) was making dinner for his family? These are the Veal & Peppers that he cooked. A dish all Italian-Americans love dearly. Wanna make it like Henry? Here you go, the recipe is right here. Enjoy!

INGREDIENTS :

24 ounces of Veal Scallopinis
2 medium Red Bell Peppers, seeded and cored
½ cup Flour
Salt & Black Pepper
12 tablespoons Olive Oil
1 tablespoon Butter

Cut the peppers in half and remove the seeds, stem, and inner core. Cut the Peppers halves into 3 equal pieces each.

Place the Peppers in a large frying pan with 8 tablespoons of olive oil and let cook at low heat until the peppers start to get soft but sill have a little firmness in them, about 25 minutes.

Remove the Peppers and their juices from the pan and set aside in a bowl.

Lay tall the Veal out and season each piece on both sides with a little Salt & Black Pepper.

Place the flour in a shallow bowl and dredge each piece of veal in the flour coating the veal on both sides. Shake off excess flour and repeat until all the veal has been dredged in flour.

Add the remaining olive oil to the pan you cooked the peppers in and turn heat to high. Once the oil is hot and the butter to the pan and let it sizzle. Add half of the veal to the pan and cook on high heat for 2 minutes on each side. Remove veal from pan and set aside, then cook remaining veal fro 2 minutes on each side as you did for the first batch.

Once the 2nd batch of veal is finished cooking, add the Peppers and all the veal to the pan and cook on low heat for two minutes.

Remove the veal from pan, placing equal portions of veal on each one of 4 plates. Divide the Peppers evenly and place on top of the veal. Pour and pan juices equally over all four portions of veal, then sprinkle chopped Parsley over the Veal & Peppers and serve.

BISTECCA ARROSTO
Italian Roast London Broil

INGREDIENTS :

¾ cup Red Wine
2 sprigs Rosemary, leaves remove from stem
3 cloves Garlic, peeled
10 tablespoons Olive Oil
2 tablespoons Baslamic Vinegar
¼ teaspoon Kosher Salt
½ teaspoon ground Black Pepper
½ teaspoon dry Oregano
2 tablespoons Dijon Mustard
1 – 1 ¾ to 2 pound Beef Shoulder London Broil
2 tablespoons Butter
¼ cup Water

Place first 9 ingredients in a Food Processor and pulse to thoroughly mixed and pureed, about 45 seconds.

Place the London Broil in a rectangular glass baking dish and pour the marinade over it. Turn the beef over so both sides are cover with the marinade. Cover with plastic wrap and put into the refrigerator and let marinate at least for 2 ½ hours or overnight, making sure to turn the meat at least two or three times so it will marinate equally on both sides.

Remove the London Broil from the refrigerator and let sit at room temperature for 1 hour before putting in the oven.

Pre-Heat the oven to 425 degrees. Put the London Broil in a steel baking pan and put into the oven. Cook the London Broil at 425 degrees until it is between Medium Rare and Medium, about 25 minutes.

Remove the London Broil and put on top of a cutting board to rest for 6-7 minutes. As the beef is resting, place the roasting pan on top of the oven and turn heat on to reduce the cooking liquid. Add a bit (1/8 to ¼ of a cup) water if you need to loosen the cooking juices a little. Once the cooking juices have reduced to a slightly thick consistency turn the heat off.

Add the butter to the pan and mix with a wooden spoon to pull the sauce into the butter.

Get 4 plates and set on the counter. Slice the London Broil on the bias to get nice ¼" thick slices and place 4 to 5 slices on each plate. Pour a bit of the sauce over each plate of London Broil and serve with Roast Potatoes and or Green Beans or other Green Vegetable and enjoy the fruits of your labors. This dish is real tasty, I'm sure you'll agree.

ROAST TUSCAN POTATOES

Roasting Potatoes in this manner is popular all over Italy, especially in Tuscany and with Sicilians. They are the perfect accompaniment for just about any grilled or roast Fish, Meat, or Poultry, and along with a Frittata or Fried Eggs for breakfast or light lunch. These potatoes are extremely versatile and should be in every good cooks repertoire. Put them in yours.

INGREDIENTS :

5 Idaho Baking Potatoes
¼ cup Olive Oil
¼ teaspoon each of Sea Salt & Black Pepper
3 sprigs fresh Rosemary
5 clove of Garlic, peeled and left whole

Wash the potatoes and cut in half long-ways. Then cut each half-potato in-half length-ways again, then cut each of these long strips into 5 pieces each. Cut each potato this way (you want cubes 1 /2 to 2" each).

Place all the ingredients except the garlic in a glass or ceramic baking dish and mix with a spoon.

Place in a 350 degree oven and bake for 20 minutes.

Add the garlic to the potatoes and mix. Cook for 15 minutes more. Take out of oven, and let set for five minutes before serving. Serve with any of the fish, meat, or poultry dish in the book.

PEPERONI ARROSTO
Italian Roast Peppers

Make these peppers and serve as an antipasto or side-dish or to top a sandwich with. Keep them in the frig and they're always ready to go. We Italians, always have them on hand, as any good Italian always should.

INGREDIENTS :

4 Red Bell Peppers
1/8 of a cup of Italian Olive Oil
4 cloves Garlic, peeled and cut in half
½ teaspoon Italian Sea Salt (or any salt you have)

Wash the peppers. Cut peppers in-half lengthwise. Remove the core, seeds, and pith from the peppers and discard. Heat oven to 325 degrees.

Pour the olive oil into a pan that's large enough to hold them in one row. Place the peppers open side up in the pan, season with half the salt and roast for 20 minutes.

Turn the peppers over to the other side and season with remaining salt. Cook for 15 minutes more, then remove from oven and let cool.

NOTE : Serve two pieces of peppers on a plate with a couple anchovy filets and you've got the famous Piedmontese Antipasto dish Peperoni al Piedmontese. Or serve as a side to any meat, fish, or poultry or on top of you Italian Hero Sandwich. Enjoy.

Danny Bolognese

EGGS & SANDWICHES

First off, everyone knows what the favorite food group of Italian-Americans is. If you don't, it's pasta. And hot on the heals depending on who your talking to, the next favorite food groups are Sandwiches or Pizza. As for me, I do love Pizza, but if I have to choose between Sandwiches and Pizza, it's not even close. For me Sandwiches are the run away winner. Pizza is great, but Id don't eat it all the time, and I can't make it at home. Sandwiches on the other had, I can whip up any time, and I'll eat a sandwich for breakfast, lunch, or dinner, or even a late night snack, I whip up an awesome sandwiches at a moments notice, and I'm dam good at it. All I need is some good bread, eggs, some cheese, and tomatoes, and if I have some Salami, Ham, Prosciutto, or Mortadella then the anti is raised all the more. If I just have some eggs and whatever cheese, I'll make you the best dam Cheese & Eggs Sandwich you ever had. I just cook up some eggs with butter & Olive Oil, make sure they're perfectly seasoned, toast the roll, and slap on the cheese and I'm good to go. If I have some tomato on hand, a couple slices will give it the finishing touch. I've published a number of sandwiches in some of my other books, so here I'll give you some new tasty ones that haven't made it into any of my books thus far. So here you go, a few of my tastiest sandwiches that I'm sure you're going to love. Buon Apettito!

SALAMI & EGG

This sandwich is absolutely awesome. It's got some bold taste with the fried Salami, which contrast well with a little Cheese, and a cool slice of ripe Tomato, and I'm sure that 99% of the people ready this have never heard of such a sandwich, but I guarantee it's sure to please.

INGREDIENTS For 4 SANDWICHES :

4 good quality Hero or Kaiser Rolls
16 slices of Sweet Sopresseta or other Salami
8 slices of Fontina or Swiss Cheese
4 large Eggs
8 Tomato Slices
Kosher or Sea Salt and Black Pepper
3 tablespoons Olive Oil
1 ½ tablespoons Butter

Slice your Rolls in half. Toast the rolls in a large non-stick frying pan, then set aside.

Place eggs in a bowl with a pinch each of Salt & Black Pepper and beat the eggs.

Turn the heat on to low and place half of the Sopresseta in the pan and let cook on very low heat for about 45 seconds. Turn the Sopresseta (Salami) over and let cook on the other side for 30 seconds (you don't want to cook too much, just heat through). Repeat with the rest of the salami. Remove the salami from the pan and set on a plate.

Place Olive Oil and Butter in the pan and turn heat to high. Once the butter start to sizzle add the eggs and cook just until the eggs are cooked through, stirring as you cook, about 3 minutes. Turn the heat off and let the eggs set in the pan.

Divide the eggs into four equal portions and place over the bottom half of four rolls. Top the eggs with equal portions of salami. Top the salami with the cheese and top the cheese with the sliced tomatoes. Season all the tomato slices with a little Salt & Pepper, then top with the top part of the rolls. Cut the sandwiches in-half and serve. There so good, just writing this is making me hungry for one. Lucky I have all the ingredients on hand to make one, and that's just what I'm going to do now. Enjoy yours, I'm going to make one now. Arreviderci!

ASPARAGUS & POTATO FRITTATA

Frittatas are one of my favorite of all Italian food items. Probably second only to pasta. I'm a bit famous for my frittata which I make often. I especially love my Sausage & Pepper Frittata, Spinach and Ricotta, and this one made with Potatoes and Asparagus. Frittatas are great to make ahead and pack into your picnic basic or take on a road trip to eat in the car whenever you get hungry, you just eat a nice little wedge of Frittata. You can serve a small piece of frittata as an antipasto course, or a larger piece with a little green salad or Caponata on the side and you all set. Learn how to make this one frittata and you'll know how to make 20 different kinds, simply by changing the filling-ingredients and cooking with the eggs.

INGREDIENTS :

1 pound Asparagus, cut off hard woody bottoms
7 large Eggs, ¼ cup grated Parmigiano Reggiano
1 Baking Potato, peeled and cut into 1" cubes
1/4 teaspoon Kosher or Sea Salt
¼ teaspoon ground Black Pepper
1 tablespoon Butter
4 tablespoons Olive Oil

Fill a medium sized pot with water and 1 tablespoon of Salt.

Cook the Asparagus in rapidly boiling water for 5 minutes. Remove with a slotted spoon or things and place in a colander, then run cold water over the Asparagus for 2 minutes to cool. Shake off excess water. Set the asparagus on a plate.
Place the potatoes in the pot and cook until just tender, about four minutes.

Remove from heat and drain the potatoes in the colander. Turn heat on to 350 degrees.

You need a 9 to 12 inch non-stick frying pan that does not have a rubber or plastic handle to cook the Frittata in the oven.

Beat the eggs in a large bowl. Add salt, pepper, cooked potatoes and asparagus and the grated cheese to the eggs and mix.
Place the olive oil and butter in your pan and place on top of a stove burner and turn the heat to high. You need to stir the eggs with a wooden spoon or spatula on high heat until the eggs are cooking and start to set but are not fully cooked yet, about 3-4 minutes. Add the pan to the oven and let your frittata finish cooking, about 6-7 minutes at 350 degrees.

Remove from oven and dislodge the frittata out of the pan and onto a large cutting board or plate. The frittata should easily slide out. If not, slide a spatula under the frittata to help get it out of the pan. Cut the frittata into wedges and serve.

NOTE : To make the Sausage & Pepper Frittata that I mention, simply cook 1 sliced Red Bell Pepper and 4 or 5 Sweet Italian Sausage links and cook them in with the eggs instead of the asparagus & potatoes and you've got yourself an awesomely tasty Sausage & Pepper Frittata. Enjoy.

FRIED MORTADELLA
The Sandwich

This sandwich, Fried Mortadella is the precursor to an All-American favorite the Fried Bologna Sandwich. One big difference, Mortadella is a superior luncheon meat to American Bologna, thus the Fried Mortadella is superior to the lowly Fried Bologna Sandwich of which I myself never like. Fried Mortadella on the other hand I absolutely love. If you ever ate Fried Bologna Sandwiches as a kid, it's time to step up and move ahead to the superior Fired Mortadella. "I dare you not to love it more!"

To MAKE ONE SANDWICH :

6 slices of Mortadella, try to get Italian Mortadella which is superior to an American one
2 slices Asiago Cheese (or Swiss or Fontina)
2 slices Tomato
Salt & Black Pepper
2 tablespoons Olive Oil
1 Hero or Kaiser Roll

Split the roll in-half and toast in a frying pan. After the roll is nice and toasted, remove from pan and place on a plate.

Cut each slice of Mortadella into 4 equal size triangular pieces. Add the Olive Oil to the pan and heat to medium-high heat. Place the Mortadella in the pan and fry them until they get a little golden color on each side of all the pieces. Place the Fried Mortadella on the bottom half of the roll. Top with the cheese, then with the slices of Tomato. Season the Tomatoes with Salt & Pepper and top with the top half of the roll. Cut the sandwich in-half and enjoy the labors of your love. Buon Apettito!

NOTE : To make 4 sandwiches, just increase the amounts of all the ingredients by four, and go to work.

NOTE II : I love the sandwich just as I've describe below, without any egg. On the other hand, I do like throwing an egg on it every now and then. If you want to, fry or scramble one egg and throw it on the middle of the above sandwich and you're good to go.

The DANNY SPECIAL

Here's a sandwich I invented one day when I had my restaurant Bar Cichetti in New York's Greenwich Village. Actually it wasn't a sandwich at first, but later on morphed into one. So one day before we about to start lunch service at the restaurant and I wanted a little something to eat, I simply fried up two Eggs and put them on a plate with 3 slices of Prosciutto. I made the plate and was walking to the bar to eat my little lunch when one of my customers stopped me and asked what I had in my hands. "Just some Fried Eggs and Prosciutto," I said, and that was that. So I had my little lunch and then went into the kitchen to cook lunch. A few minutes later one of my waitresses cam into the kitchen and asked me if I cam make Fried Eggs & Prosciutto for the customer who had seen me with the plate. "Sure," I told her. A minute later she cam back and asked if I could make some Garlic Bread to go with the Prosciutto & Eggs? Sure," again. So I made the plate, the guy ate it and loved it, and he'd come in all the time and I'd make for him. One day he stopped in and said he was in rush, and could I make him his normal Prosciutto and Eggs but instead of on a plate, could I make it into a sandwich for him? You know the answer by now don't you? "Sure!" So that's how this tasty little sandwich came to be, a spur of the moment thing that was totally random, but wonderful none-the-less.

ITALIAN HOT DOG

An Italian Hot Dog you want to know? What is it? Well it's a Jersey thing, and you're not gonna find them anywhere else other the in-and-around Newark, New Jersey and some of the towns surround it. Burgers and Hot Dogs are really big in Jersey and there once was a guy named James "Buff" Racioppi who first served this thing called the Italian Hot Dog. James and his Italian Buddy's used to have many a card game in Newark's 9th Ward way back when. One day Jimmy's wife threw together something for her husband and card playing cronies to eat. She fried up some Sweet Bell Peppers, Potato, Onions, and Hot Dogs, and when everything was finished frying she put it all between some bread and served it to all the hungry card players. Well everyone just loved the sandwiches and whenever they played cards they begged for her to make the Italian Style Hot Dogs. These Hot Dogs were so popular and everyone just love them that Jimmy decide to open a little stand and sell them. You know the rest, the Italian Hot Dogs were a huge success and Jimmy Buffs Hot Dog empire was born (1932 in Newark, New Jersey).

And oh by the way, Jimmy Buff Racioppi is the one who always gets credit for inventing this awesome culinary delight, but the real inventor was Jimmy's wife Mrs. Racioppi.

My Dad used to take use to all the Diners, Hot Dog & Burger Joints around. We'd go to Jimmy Buffs maybe 3 or 4 times a year. My mom learned how to make these tasty Italian Hot Dogs and we'd have them at least once a month when we couldn't make it down to Jimmy Buffs. My mom made them so good, they were just as good as Jimmy Buffs. Now you can make them too.

INGREDIENTS :

4 Hero Rolls
1 small Red Bell Pepper and one Green, seeded and sliced
2 medium Onions, peeled and sliced
8 best quality Hot Dogs
2 Idaho Potatoes, peeled and slice ¼" thick
Salt & Black Pepper
¼ cup Canola Oil

Place the potatoes in a small pot of water. Add 1 tablespoon Salt. Bring the water to a boil and cook the potatoes at the boil for 2 minutes. Turn heat off and drain the potatoes in a colander, shaking off as much water as possible.

Add 1/3 of the oil to a medium frying pan. Turn heat on to medium and add the Hot Dogs. Fry the Hot Dogs until they get golden brown and crunchy on all sides, about 8-10 minutes. Turn heat off and leave in pan covered with aluminum foil.

Place the ¾ of the oil in a large frying pan and heat to high. Put the potatoes in the frying pan and season with a little salt & Black Pepper and fry the potatoes on high heat for 6 minutes. Add the Bell Pepper to the pan, turn down the heat and cook the peppers with the potatoes on low heat for 10 minutes, stirring as you cook. Add the onions, season with Salt & Pepper and cook the onions with the Peppers & Potatoes over low heat for 8 minutes.

Put the Hot Dogs in with the Peppers, Onions, & Potatoes and cook on very low heat for 2 minutes. In the mean time, split the rolls in half but not all the way through, leaving a sort of hinge on one side of each roll. Place in the pan that the Hot Dogs cooked in, turn heat on to high and toast the rolls until they get a little crunchy.

Place two Hot Dogs on each roll and fill each roll with some of the Peppers, Onions, & Potatoes mixture. Serve to your buddy's and enjoy.

The HALF & HALF

The half & half is even better that the regular Italian Hot Dog. To make one, instead of putting 2 Hot Dogs in each roll with the Peppers, Onions, & Potatoes, you cook up some Italian Sausages and put one Hot Dog and one Sausage Link into each roll with the Potato, Onions, and Peppers and you're all set with a Italian Hot Dog Half & Half. You're gonna Love It!

RICOTTA CHEESECAKE

My cookbooks aren't usually big on desserts. If you want to get a cookbook that has a lot of dessert recipes in it, there are many out there. When I cook for friends and family, I usually don't cook dessert as I concentrate on the Meat & Bones of the meal, the savory food, and I usually get one of the guests to bring some sweets. And we do love having a little bit of sweets at all our little dinner parties, it's just that I don't often make any, though every once and a while I'll make an Orange Cake, or this one, everyone's favorite Ricotta Cheesecake. So I've included the recipe here below, and I think you will like it.

INGREDIENTS:

2 lbs. whole milk Ricotta
6 extra large Eggs
¾ cup Sugar
zest of 2 Lemon and 1 Oranges
1/8 teaspoon of Salt
1 teaspoon Vanilla Extract
4 tablespoons flour
1-2 cup plain breadcrumbs & 2 tablespoons Sugar
Butter (to grease pan)

Grease a 9" spring-form pan with butter. Mix breadcrumbs and 2 tablespoons of sugar together. Place mixture in buttered pan. Move breadcrumb mixture around to coat pan with mixture.

Beat eggs with ¾ cup of sugar. Add vanilla, and Lemon & Orange Zest if using. Add flour and continue beating ingredients together. Little by little, add the Ricotta to bowl and mix until all the ricotta is incorporated and smooth.

Heat oven to 375 degrees.

Place the spring-form pan inside a large pan. Pour all of the Ricotta (Cheesecake) mixture inside the spring-form pan. Pour warm water into the larger pan that is holding the spring-form pan with the ricotta mixture. Pour water half way up the sides of the spring-form pan. This is a water-bath.

Bake for 15 minute at 375 degrees. Turn oven down to 325 degree and bake cheesecake for 50 to 60 minutes more, until when you put a toothpick into the center of the cake, it comes out clean.

Cool cheesecake for 1 hour outside at room temperature. Place cheesecake in refrigerator and cook for 2 to 3 hours before serving.

Danny Bolognese

TIRAMISU

Tiramisu, what is it, what does it mean? Well in this day and age, just about every American knows what Tiramisu is, it's a tasty Italian dessert that's made with Espresso, Italian Lady Fingers (Savaoiardi) and a smooth lush custard made of Marscapone Cream. So what does it mean. Tiramisu means "pick me up" a reference to Espresso Coffee that as everyone knows has a stimulant affect of waking one up, a reason billions drink coffee first thing in the morning each and every day. Tiramisu originated in the Veneto in the city of Treviso at the restaurant Le Biccherie. It quickly gained popularity in the tourist mad city of Venice where tourist from the United States and all over the World ate it and loved it, and little by little its popularity spread all of the World, thus making it one of the worlds most ubiquitous and popular desserts of all.

INGREDIENTS :

4 tablespoons Instant Espresso
1 /34 cups o Boiling Hot Water
½ cup Sugar
4 tablespoons Kahlua or Tia Maria (Coffee Liqueur)
4 Egg Yolks
¾ cup Sweet Marsala Wine
1 cup Heavy Cream

1 pound Marscapone Cheese (room temperature and soft)
40 Savaoiardi Biscuits (Italian Ladyfingers)
Cocoa Powder (for dusting the top of the Tiramisu)

Put the Instant Espresso and 2 tablespoons of Sugar in the boiling water and mix.

Place the Egg Yolks and Marsala with the remaining sugar in a large Stainless Steele bowl. Get a small pot and put in two cups of water and bring to a simmer. Place the SS Bowl over the pot with simmering water (Double Boiler) and beat the eggs at high speed with a electric mixer until the contents triples in volume, about 4-5 minutes.

Add the Marscapone into the Egg / Marsala mixture gently, adding a little at a time, folding into the eggs until all the Marscapone is incorporated into the eggs.

Beat the Heavy Cream until they form peaks. Fold the Whipped Cream into the Marscapone mixture until all is incorporated.

Get a 9" X 13" glass or ceramic baking pan that you will make the Tiramisu in. One by one, dip the Savaoiardi Biscuits into the espresso, holding for about 5 seconds to let the espresso soak into the biscuit just a little but not too much. Place the soaked biscuit to start one of two long rows that will be side-by-side to fill the pan in two long neat rows. Repeat this process until you fill the bottom of the pan with the Espresso Soaked Savaoiardi.

Spread half of the Marscapone mixture over the Biscuites, then make another layer of soaked Savaoiardi over the marscapone.

Place remaining marscapone over the second layer of biscuits. Take Cocoa Powder and put in a wire sieve and shake over the top of the Tiramisu to completely dust the top with Coco.

Place in the refrigerator for two to three hours before serving.

NOTE : If you like, you can make fresh brewed Espresso instead of the instant Espresso, which would be great, but either way is fine and you'll have some nice tasty Tiramisu for you and your guests.

TORTA CAPRESE

If you want to make your own dessert, but nothing to complicated, then Torta Caprese from the beautiful Isle of Capri is the dessert for you. It's super easy to make, it happens to be delicious, and most of your friends will probably never have had it before, so it makes for a nice unexpected little surprise at the end of the meal. Now how can you beat that? You can't, so make it and enjoy.

INGREDIENTS :

1 ½ sticks Butter
good quality Dark Chocolate
½ cup Sugar
¾ cup Brown Sugar
6 Eggs
1 teaspoon Almond Extract
1 Cup ground Almonds (or Walnuts) Grind in a food Processor
1 tablespoon Flour
1 ½ tablespoon Cocoa
Powder Sugar for dusting finished Cake

Grease a 9-inch cake pan with butter. Turn oven on to 350 degrees.

Place the butter in a small pot and melt the butter over a low flame. Remove pot from heat and immediately add the Chocolate. Mix the chocolate with a rubber spatula until it completely melts. Let cool for 8 minutes.

Place Eggs, Sugar, Brown Sugar, and almond extract and beat vigorously.

Add the flour, ground Almonds, and Coca to the chocolate and mix thoroughly to a smooth consistency.

Add this batter to the greased cake pan. Place pan in the oven and bake the torta until when you stick a toothpick in the center it will come out clean, about 40-45 minutes.

Remove the Torta Caprese from the oven and set on the counter to cool for at least 15 minutes before serving. Serve with Powdered 10x Sugar sprinkled over the top, and your all set to go. Or for a little bit more embellishment serve with whipped cream and fresh berries. Enjoy.

BUDINO di RISO
Italian Rice Pudding

If you want to make a nice refreshing dessert that's easy to make and can be made ahead the day before you're going to have a dinner party, this Italian Rice Pudding is a great choice.

INGREDIENTS :

2 cups Arborio Rice
2 ½ cups of Milk
½ cup Sugar, 3 large Eggs, beaten
1 tablespoon melted Butter
1/8 teaspoon Salt, Zest of 1 Orange
¼ cup Raisons
¼ teaspoon each of Cinnamon and Nutmeg

Place 4 quarts of water in a 6 quart pot and bring to the boil. Add the rice and boil for 14 minutes. Remove from heat and strain the rice in a wire-strainer. Run cold water over and into the rice for 5 minutes. Shake off excess water and let the rice sit and cool for 12 minutes.

Place the beaten Eggs, Milk, Salt, melted Butter, Raisons, and Orange Zest in a large bowl and mix. Add the rice and mix.

Turn oven on to 350 degrees. Place the rice into a 9" X 13" Pyrex baking pan and bake in the oven at 350 degrees for 20 minutes. Remove from the oven and let cool on the counter. Sprinkle Cinnamon and Nutmeg over the top of the pudding and put into the refrigerator at least 3 hours before serving.

PARTY alla BOLOGNESE

Party alla Bolognese, ever hear of it? No, I didn't think so. I coined the phrase, just like I coined the phrase Meatball Parm Mondays, which I first wrote about in my best selling Italian Cookbook Sunday Sauce. So, you want to know what a *Party alla Bolognese* is, a term you are no doubt hearing for the first time. Well as you might have already surmised, number one, it's a party that has to do with Bolognese. A party where you eat Pasta with Ragu Bolognese you're asking? Well yes, you are quite correct, you'll be eating the famed Italian Ragu from the city of Bologna, Italy. This is a party centered around eating Pasta all Bolognese. Now what's better than that?

So, as we know Ragu Bolognese is the famous meat-sauce for pasta from Bologna, Italy. Now, hopefully by the time you read this part of the book, you've already made your first Ragu alla Bolognese. Well congratulations are in order to you, you've learned something that is infinitely important, and something that *will serve you the rest of your life.* You now know the *infinite glories of the Bolognese*, that lush pasta meat-sauce from Bologna, Italy, Ragu Bolognese. You know the wonderful flavor, and are sure to crave it often. No problem, if you have a craving, you can just make it. You have the recipe, you've made it once or twice, you can make it any time you want.

So, you want to throw a dinner party for friends? I certainly hope you do. If you've never done so before, I'd just like to tell you, you have no idea, and I'm sure you'll be surprised.

Making a this famed Ragu and throwing a party centered around the Bolognese where you'll feed Maccheroni alla Bolognese to friends in family, this is such a wonderful thing, you just can't imagine. Do it once and you'll see. You will make your friends oh-so-happy in more ways than one. They will thank you and sing your praises, and you will feel their joy. A joy that you gave them by making them Ragu Bolognese. Yes it has this affect.

Throwing a dinner party you say? It seems so daunting. Hey, you've made Bolognese, throwing a dinner party centered around Bolognese is as easy as pie, and I'm going tell you how. You will amaze your friends with this one! Trust me! Hey, I've already told you pretty much, 90% of all you'll need to know to do your first fabulous Party alla Bolognese. "What," you say? Well I've written the recipe for you, and you've already made your first Bolognese, maybe even two or three by now. You know how to make one of the World's great *dishes* Pasta alla Bolognese, all you need now is some good music, good Italian Wine, and some sort of Salad or Antipasto to start you off.

You will make the Bolognese ahead of time, either the day before or early in the day before your party starts. You can either make a salad to have before the Bolognese, but a better choice would be either a Caprese Salad of fresh Mozzarella & Tomatoes, a lovely mixed Antipasto, or something as easy as Prosciutto & Melon would be very apropos, considering the Bolognese and the famed Prosciutto di Parma are both from the same region in Italy of Emilia Romagna.

So you go out and get some Provolone or other cheese if you're going to serve a mixed antipasto before the Bolognese. Get some good Sweet Sopresseta, a jar of good quality Roast Red Peppers, and the best Italian Olives you can get, and your mixed antipasto is all set. Tell each guest to bring a nice bottle of Italian Wine, unless you prefer to buy the wine yourself, it's all up to you. And there is nothing wrong with your guests each bringing a bottle. When they do so you end up getting a nice variety of different wines to taste, making your party not just a Party alla Bolognese but a pleasant little wine tasting as well. Nice, no? Yes, this works out quite well, and it makes the party a little more interesting, tasting the different wines. Tell your friends to bring Chianti, Barbera, Montepulciano di Abruzzo, or Lambrusco which is from Emilia Romagna and is the perfect wine if you're having either Prosciutto & Melon or a Mixed Antipasto with some nice Salumi and Cheese to start.

You've got to have some nice background music for your party. The best music would be a mix of first and foremost Frank Sinatra, with Dean Martin, a little Tony Bennett, and some Louis Prima to boot. Hip Hop and Heavy Metal are strictly forbidden and an absolute no-no, you don't want to ruin your party with bad music, do you?

Dessert and coffee are always great. They are not an absolute must, but I do highly recommend you serve coffee and dessert. Again, you may want to have one or two of your friends pick up some dessert. Italian desserts like: Ricotta Cheesecake, Italian Pastries and or Cookies, or Gelato are all great, but not absolutely necessary that the dessert be Italian. Maybe one of your friends makes a great Pineapple Upside Down Cake, a Red Velvet Cake or something like that is great. What's important is you have a dessert, it's just another little facet of your dinner party, your Party alla Bolognese. And don't forget the Bolognese is the centerpiece and as they say in France *The Piece de Resistance*!

PARTY alla BOLOGNESE CHECKLIST

1. Get your ingredients for the Bolognese; the ground meat you choose. Tomatoes, wine, pasta, milk, butter, Olive Oil, and dry Porcini Mushrooms if you decide to use them.

2. Get your ingredients for your Antipasto course.

3. Buy at least two bottles of good Italian Wine, even if you have your guest bring wine, you'll still want to get at least two bottles of your own.

4. Have plenty of spring or filtered water. Buy gallons of Spring Water (at least 2 gallons or more).

5. Buy one or two loaves of good Italian Bread.

6. Make the Bolognese! It's great to make the night before the party. Just to let you know, it doesn't hurt that the Bolognese is made the night before, it's actually better.

7. Make sure you have some great music; Sinatra, Tony Bennett, or mellow R&B music.

8. Before your guest arrive, get your antipasto or salad ready to go when you need it. Keep it simple. If you choose one of the antipasto items from the antipasto section in this book, you can't go wrong, they're all real simple and don't require any cooking, other than if you choose the Shrimp Cocktail, which is super simple and takes just a few minutes and can be done ahead of time, a few hours before or the day before your party.

9. A few minutes before you will be serving the antipasto, put your pot of Bolognese on the stove and turn the heat onto the lowest flame possible to heat up your Bolognese. If after the Bolognese is simmering for twenty minutes, it looks like it is getting dry out, you can add some water.

10. Put a large pot of water on to cook the pasta. Put a lot of salt in the pasta cooking water.

11. Serve the antipasto course with your guest and make sure have some nice Sinatra tunes playing. Enjoy the antipasto with your guest.

12. Turn the water for the pasta on to a high flame. After you have eaten your antipasto with your guest wait a about 15 or more before you serve the Bolognese.

13. Rigatoni, Cavatappi, Fusilli, or some sort of short pasta are the best type of pasta to serve with your Ragu Bolognese at Party alla Bolognese party, as it's easy to serve and to eat than a long pasta like Spaghetti or Tagiatelle for your guest. Got that? Serve a short pasta.

14. After everyone has eaten their antipasto and are enjoying their wine, throw the pasta in the water to cook. The pasta will take about 12 minutes to cook. You want to have about 20 minutes in-between the antipasto and Bolognese course, so throw the pasta in the boiling water 10 minutes after everyone has finished eating.

15. Follow the directions for cooking the pasta that is on the pasta package. Once the pasta is finished cooking, drain the pasta in a colander, reserving about a ¼ cup of the pasta cooking liquid. Add the pasta back to the pot that it cooked in. Add some of the Bolognese with a couple knobs of butter to the pot and mix the pasta and Bolognese Sauce together. Have a plate ready for each guest and plate each one with an equal portion of the Pasta Bolognese. Serve to your guest and make sure to pass around grated cheese.

Ragu Bolognese Cookbook

DO LIKE THE ITALIANS

For those of you who may not know, Italians in Italy do not usually eat dessert at home with a normal family dinner. Quite often after the main course is eaten in an Italian Family home in Italy, Italians like to eat not dessert but some nice fresh seasonal fruit. Most popular are fresh seasonal Cherries and Watermelon. Italians also might have some fresh Peaches or Apricots as well. If they do have desserts, Italians are likely to go out to a local Gelateria for Gelato or to a famous Pasticceria for cookies, cake or pastries with Espresso.

So if you like, get a nice fresh Watermelon, slice it up and pass it around after your tasty soul satisfying Bolognese. The watermelon is sweet, juicy, and refreshing and a nice way to finish a Party Bolognese or whatever your savory theme dish might be. If you get Cherries, wash them and put into a bowl with iced water, and put the bowl of Cherries in the water in the middle of the table for everyone to grab. Make sure you have a little bowl to throw the pits into.

You can finish the meal off just like this, but you're probably not. Most Italians want a little Espresso afterwards, so if you have a Moka or Napoletana Coffee Pot for making espresso, then you must do so.

Place a bottle of Anisette or Sambucca on the table to pour a little into the espresso to make a Caffe Corretto, or drink the Anisette or Sambucca out of little cordial glasses. A few Biscotti Cookies on the side wouldn't hurt as well. Enjoy, you're Italian! Or at least eating like one.

GRAZIE MILLE

Thank you so much for getting this book. I do hope you *enjoyed* it, learn from it and *use it over and over again* for many *wonderful times* making meals for your friends, family, and loved ones. And keep in mind that this book was written and based on and around, as you know by now the awesomely delightful and quite possibly the world's most wonderful dish, *Ragu Bolognese*. Also keep in mind that along with the Bolognese, the book is a compact condensed little cookbook of Italian-America's *favorite* and *most beloved dishes*. The dishes within comprise the core-nucleus of this beloved cuisine of which all Americans love dearly, be they Italian or not, you can always enjoy the greatness of the Italian Table. If you get the message I'm driving at, this book can be the nucleus of years of these delightful meals. It's the *perfect beginner Italian Cookbook*, short, simply, and wonderful. You don't have to learn a lot. Get famous for your; Marinara, your, Bolognese, and maybe a soup or two. Perfect these dishes and you will be a Rock Star in your circle of friends. Yes you will.

So Thanks Again
e
Mille Grazie,

Daniele

MANGIA BENE !!!

Danny Bolognese

by The Same Author

SUNDAY SAUCE
When Italian-Americans Cook

THE FEAST of THE 7 FISH
Italian Christmas

SEGRETO ITALIANO
Secret Italian Recipes

GRANDMA BELLINO COOKBOOK
Recipes From My Sicilian Grandmother

La TAVOLA
*Italian New Yorkers Adventures
of The Table*

Danny Bolognese

CONGRADULATIONS
YOU KNOW HOW to MAKE a BOLOGNESE
The WORLD'S GREATEST DISH of ALL
MANY THINKS SO
IT'S LUSH COMFORTING
And Oh So TATSY
THE BOLOGNESE

YOU'RE A PRINCE AMONG MEN
YOU KNOW The SECRETS of The
BOLOGNESE
GO FORTH And MAKE IT
TREAT YOUR FAMILY
YOUR FRIENSDS

IT'S BOLOGNESE
And THERE'S NOT MANY THINGS BETTER

Danny Bolognese

Danny Bolognese

BASTA la PASTA !!!!!